THOSE SUMMER DAYS

SHIRLEY PORTER

Those Summer Days

Copyright © 2022 Shirley Porter

All rights reserved. No part of this publication may be reproduced or transmitted in any form or by any means without the written permission of the publisher.

All rights reserved.

ISBN: 978-1-956884-09-8

Contributing Editor: or all services completed
by Imprint Productions, Inc.
Cover Design: or all services completed
by Imprint Productions, Inc.

Printed in the United States of America
Published by Imprint Productions, Inc.
First Edition 2022

DEDICATION

I would like to dedicate this book to my sister Norma, and my twin sister, Sandra. They are no longer with us, and I miss them dearly. Special thanks to my husband, Bernett Sr. for his support and my big sister Elizabeth, who is very much a part of this adventure. Extra special thanks to my oldest son, Bernett Jr., who would constantly remind me to finish this book. My two children Deshonna and Levi who are also no longer with us, they both hold an extra special place in our hearts that especially helps get me through the hard times. The memories we shared were happy times and will last forever.

ACKNOWLEDGEMENT

This book came into being for the people in my life. With great love for each of them: Professor Judith Mayton, my teacher, sister in Christ, a friend, someone I could vent and get angry when she would tell me the truth, who struck with me and did not allow me to give-up when my world was falling apart. She suggested I write my feelings and most enjoyable times on paper. Wow! This is the second book, and I am continuing the journey! Many thanks to Dr. Mayton, and her husband, who did not mind her sharing some of her time with me.

Professor Diane Frazier, who wrapped her arms around me, and shed tears with my tears, along with my pain. You are so precious to me, and I cannot thank you enough.

Professor Virginia Spears, who helped me, and gave her ear to listen to my every word. Thank you for the thoughts, the shared prayers and support when my brain seemed to be dull.

My family: Little Bernett (oldest son) and my love who always would call and ask, "Where's the book mom?" My two darling children who are resting in His arms. We miss you (Levi and Deshonna). My three children enjoyed and explored the world outside and the many things around them. They found the simple pleasures of summer.

The family: my twin sister Sandra (Sandy) and Norma, who we miss dearly, Liz and me. All of the children on our street are a part of this great adventure. I could not have written this story without them. To Tracy, Joyce, Phyllis, Shirnea, and the little ones, thank you for being there when I needed someone to love and help me get through some of the hard times. Thank you Bernett for believing in me when I was afraid to believe in myself. Those hidden resources helped through the pain.

To God, who blessed me with two more children to raise in my older age, "Thank you," Jeremiah, my grandson and Tanneesha, my niece.

PREFACE

An adventure does not have to happen in a faraway place. It can happen right where you are, just outside in the yard. Children can use the creative abilities that lie just between their mind and the natural world.

This book is for those who are young and those who are young at heart. It will bring back fond memories for those of us who can look back at those early days of summer and remember the lazy-haze days with the friends we met. Summer days were when we had fun outside, even on those quick rainy days. Those days when the neighborhood was the jungle, and the dogs and cats were the wild animals. The sidewalk was the speedway, our place to race up and down on. Where you found simple, creative ways to enjoy the day. It will encourage today's children to put away technical toys and gadgets for a minute and find that adventure right outside your door. Enjoying being a kid in "Those Summer Days."

TABLE OF CONTENTS

INTRODUCTION:	1
CHAPTER I: THOSE SUMMER DAYS	5
CHAPTER II: WHAT IS GOING ON?	9
CHAPTER III: MARY JO AND HER OLD TRICKS	14
CHAPTER IV: THE MOVE THAT SHOCKED THE GROUP	18
CHAPTER V: THE GANG IN DISBELIEF	21
CHAPTER VI: SUNDAY MORNING	24
CHAPTER VII: THE SWEET AROMA	27
CHAPTER VIII: A MOST NEEDED RIDE	30
CHAPTER IX: LOOKING FOR MARY JO	33
CHAPTER X: HOME AT LAST	36
CHAPTER XI: LOOKING FOR BILLYRAY?	40
CHAPTER XII: MASON JAR	43
CHAPTER XIII: AFTER WE GET THE MONEY	47
CHAPTER XIV: POP BOTTLES AND SCRAP METAL	51
CHAPTER XV: GOING TO MR. BOB'S STORE	54
CHAPTER XVI: GIRL AND A CAT NAMED TOM	59
CHAPTER XVII: TO CLOSE FOR COMFORT	64
CHAPTER XIII: MARY JO MISBEHAVING	67
CHAPTER XIX: MARY JO BIG SCARE	70
CHAPTER XX: THE SUMMER HEAT	73
CHAPTER XXI: HERE COME THE MENFOLK	77
CHAPTER XXII: THE FISH FRY	80
CHAPTER XXIII: HOW MUCH MONEY DID WE MAKE	86
CHAPTER XXIV: B. J. S' OVERNIGHT STAY	90
CHAPTER XXV: FRIEND'S FOREVER ENJOYING THE QUIETNESS	93
CHAPTER XXVI: AFRICAN JUNGLE HUNT	97
CHAPTER XXVII: WHERE ARE THE BOYS	102
CHAPTER XXVIII: GOING TO GET THE TWINS	106
CHAPTER XXIX: THE TWIN'S GIFT TO THEIR FRIEND	110

INTRODUCTION

Here we go again, finding ourselves where we left off, in this little town called Johnson City, Tennessee. Those of you who do not have the first book are missing what this book entails. The five little characters and some of the towns' people play an important role in this story. My first book leaves the readers with a cliffhanger. Billy Ray, one of the main characters, left us wondering about a big secret, but he did not reveal it. On the other hand, another series had to be written to reveal "Billy Ray's Big Secret," which made his friend nervous. Mary Jo is struggling with what that boy is holding from the group. Nevertheless, you will find out in this book. The creative adventures that will heighten your imagination as you become a part of what these children are discovering.

Simple pleasure was something their leader and sometimes the boys would share. In the new series, "Those Summer Days," the characters are finding ways to make money and determining what to do with it. They learn how to rekindle friendships, share, grow from hurt feelings, and discover new paths. They even receive gifts from the twins. These are just a few things that these five little people did.

"Those Summer Days" highlights each character's behavior when faced with adversity: the tears, the pain, setbacks, bullying, teasing, and forgiveness. As you will see, these characters are not perfect, and all learn a lesson in respecting each other's feelings.

Despite many battles and wars, these children did not let the war affect them. In fact, they watched films about World War II, which they were all born into. Although they are aware of potential obstacles due to their race, they chose to do their own thing.

They did not need technology for their brains to click. They chose to use the resources that lay dormant within them, to bring out the best in them which could influence whatever they enjoyed discovering.

Every day they got together was an adventure. They enjoyed their summer vacation and remembered the good times they had as kids. So, when asked by the grandkids or younger people, "What did you do in the summertime?" You can happily smile and say, "It was fun, fun, fun."

It does not cost a dime to go outside like these five little characters are doing. Life will be better and who knows; you are never too old to be the next Author. I will be 80 years old when this book comes out. Stir up your curiosity & come join the children. Happy reading!

Just inside the Tennessee border is a little town that is so back in the boonies that folks say it fell off the map. Hardly anyone could find it. Johnson City is nestled like a baby, in a valley that's surrounded by majestic mountains that seem to tower the soft blue skies and the fluffy white clouds. A pictorial scene of beautiful rolling hills, fresh springs flowing down the mountainside and a patchwork quilt of the farmland as far as the eyes can see.

Even before you come into the little downtown area, you can hear the big fountain splashing in the middle of the square. The two old black wrought iron benches, with planks for seats, surround a tall pole wrapped in honeysuckle vines that fill the air with wild sweetness. Near the top of this pole, there are two flags blowing in the wind. Adults come to get the entire town's latest gossip and little ears hear, "Go feed the pigeons that gather round for a free meal."

Across the street, there are red, brick sidewalks that will take you to the town's main stores such as Park-N-Belt Store, Bob's Drug Store, Minnie's Boy & Girl's Shop, and Kens' Shoe Store. Farther up Main Street is the fashionable Mark's, where only the rich people could afford to shop. Just around the corner is the Five and Dime, where anyone could go. Next, is Harvey's Shoes Shop, The Sears's Catalog Store, and 2 theaters - one for the colored and one for whites only. Ford's Appliance Store is a bit farther down, followed by the Southern Pacific Train Station, 2 bus stations - The Greyhound Bus Station and Trail Way Bus Station, as well as Bud's Hamburger Stand (the best hamburger your mouth ever tasted).

Dunbar Elementary is a school built some forty years ago for the colored folks, and it sits on the other side of the tracks. For such an old school, it has an enormous amount of character. Its weather beaten, red bricks on the outside show no fear of the elements that have assaulted it throughout the years. The school building starts at the corner of Elm Street and ends on the corner of Popular Street. Two large Elm trees sit on each side of the entrance, their leaves swaying lazily in the breeze.

Old-timers like Mr. Sam, Mr. Bob, Old Toothless Slim and several others stop for a spell under the shady trees to play a game of checkers, or dominos, but mostly, to reminisce about years gone by. If you like listening to old stories, this was the place to be. Every now and then, Mr. Sam would pull out his handkerchief and with his tired, black hand, he'd wipe the sweat from his brow while slowly telling his tale. Toothless Slim responds with "Ah-hum" to everything said. Mr. Bob sits quietly on an apple crate fanning himself and chewing Beechnut Tobacco, while reminding Slim "it's yo move, Ah-hum."

As the season changes from summer to fall, colored leaves put on a show, glittering in the morning dew. Mother Nature blows her frosty breath, sending the leaves scurrying across the barren ground. Children's laughter would fill the air as they jumped and romped in the leaves piled as high as the sky.

Sometimes, Mr. Bob and his dog Rover would sit on the old cobble steps just passing the time away. Mr. Bob watches the children play while Rover barks and tries to catch leaves before they hit the ground. Rover likes linear cobble steps and large doors with glass panes and faded wooden frames. With his nose pressed against the glass, he can see the old screenless windows decorated with wild honeysuckle vines growing around their battered frames. Every now and then, you can taste the scent of the wildflowers. Flies and bees were about their business enjoying the sweet nectar that these flowers had to give.

In the back of the schoolyard, is one big sliding board sitting in the shadow of the building. This would keep the sliding board from getting hot from the afternoon sun. Four swings held aloft with large, looping chains that suspended from big steel rods. The chains make a loud clanging sound as children swing as high as they can go. Cool wind whips across their faces, tears of joy fill their eyes and little voices sing, "Wee! Wee!" When recess was over, they paid 'no never mind' to the swings' wooden seats, as they rubbed their splintered behinds.

On the other side of the schoolyard, boys play with a rounded stick and a rubber ball on the tightly packed red clay. You can hear them yell, "hit that ball" as the batter would swing with all his might, trying to imitate his favorite baseball player. His teammate would holler, "It's a homerun", as the rubber ball soared up and out of the yard.

Finally, the day comes for excited sixth graders to move on. This was the day to say goodbye to all the teachers, young schoolmates, and elementary school days. Although they are happy to leave it behind, they will carry fond memories of the weather-beaten old building that stood the test of time. They think about what lies ahead - the good times they'll have and the new friends they'll meet. The silly songs, the quiet time, and the many games they will play. Winter has passed and summer is near where days are filled with delight as the fireflies dance in the night.

So come along and get on board to fill your heart with a tale you might like. Oh! The joy of being a kid in the summertime time, where your imagination runs wild to discover life's joy and a little pain. Just right outside your doors, you find your dreams, in the good ole' summertime.

CHAPTER I
THOSE SUMMER DAYS

Mary Jo quickly sat up in the bed, as if frightened by a dream. She sat wide-eyed, as she suddenly realized Billy Ray would be leaving with his family in six days. The gang would lose one of its weirdest members. In an instant, Mary Jo began to lose control of her senses. She inadvertently stopped and said, "What am I doing! I should be overjoyed that the pest, Billy Ray, is going away. After all, he has embarrassed Mary Jo on several occasions. Once, he was acting like an airplane in front of his house, making that annoying noise with his mouth.

Immediately, she came to herself and with a smirk look on her face, she reminded herself, "Hum! I do not have to listen to Billy Ray rant and rave about them 'darn' old planes anymore. Oops! My Gosh" Mary Jo hysterically said. "Listen to what I just let pass my lips!" Quickly she put her hands over her mouth as if to erase the word 'darn.' She thought, "I have just used a bad word again."

Dumbfounded as guilt infiltrated her little mind Mary Jo went from good to worse. "OOOH! If my mama heard me say a bad word such as that, she would give me the "What fors!" Mary Jo, being tormented by saying 'darn', hurried to the bathroom. In the closed confines of the bathroom, she escaped her fears. Looking in the old mirror that hung from a braided rope over the sink, she ran some water. Without hesitating, she quickly washed her tongue until she felt it was clean. Then she washed her face and the nightmares off her body.

Next, she reached for her toothbrush that was in a tin cup, as she dreaded brushing her teeth. Mrs. Hattie refused to buy toothpaste because baking soda was better than that sweet paste. Looking in the mirror as she rinsed out her mouth, she said "mama just like buying that old nasty tasting baking soda because it cost a nickel."

However, as her pickled mind changed at that moment, she began to practice her speech for Billy Ray on Friday night. The gang did not ask her to be their spokesperson, she just took upon her smart self to deliver the going away speech. Knowing that she was the smartest in the gang, Mary Jo put her hand over her brow, tilted her head back, put one foot out in front of the other one and began her speech. She already practiced for the twins when she was at their house. Very arrogantly, she said, "I know, without a doubt, that one of the boys at school will be glad to take your place, Billy Ray Sims. Seeing that it was my responsibility to come up with most of the stuff we did this summer."

"Oh!" Mary Jo said as if she had forgotten something she should have said. Pacing around the bathroom and catching a glimpse of her expression in the mirror she continued her speech. "Billy Ray do not fret! You know ah rah! Let me see, the fact is ah rah!" She was having trouble getting her words together. However, she finally said, "Billy Ray, the gang has had some good times with you. We pray that you will enjoy your new home. The gang will always be down here. Oh, and just remember, Billy Ray, it won't be a problem filling your spot. Knowing you are one of our members, the church ladies will serve you the first plate Friday night. Thank you!" Mary Jo took a bow as if she had just given a commencement speech. She has really outdone herself this time. The gang did not pick her to speak for them. She was just over acting again, like she usually does.

In the meantime, she decided to get dressed as her mama called out for her to come to breakfast. "Come on child, your breakfast is getting cold," Mrs. Hattie said. Mary Jo called from the bathroom that she would be right down. After such a performance, she felt hunger pains roaming around in her stomach. She hurried and finished dressing. Hurrying out into the hallway with the intention of riding the railing down the stairs, she was surprised to see Mrs. Hattie standing at the bottom of the stairs.

"Uh Hum!" Mrs. Hattie said as she pointed her finger at Mary Jo. "Yoes better walk down dem stairs like a lady! God made dem legs for yoes to walk with. Yoes hear me, Mary Jo Ruth Finney?"

By the time she reached the bottom step, Mary Jo knew she better have a good answer. Very poised and acting the part of an actor, Mary Jo got to the bottom step and said, "Mama! What is that making my eyes water, my nose sniffing the air like a hungry hound-dog, and my mouth taste that good aroma and the scent of something special?"

All Mrs. Hattie could do was laugh and say, "Mary Jo, goin in de kitchen, child." The smell from the food made Mary Jo's stomach growl even louder. "Hum, hum!" She said, as she sat down in her favorite seat by the window. Mrs. Hattie did not waste any time serving biscuits, country ham in red gravy, one sunny-side-up egg, blackberry jam, and a cold glass of milk in her other hand. She thanked her mama as she began to eat. Mary Jo was eating so fast that her mama had to intervene.

"Mary Jo, where are your manners, girl? Yoes knows better than dat."

Mary Jo timidly said, "Mama, I am sorry," wiping her mouth with the back of her hand. Mrs. Hattie refused to say another word to Mary Jo and politely gave her a cup towel. "Oh! I forgot to get one mama" Mary Jo said.

At that moment, Mary Jo's thoughts were not on Billy Ray. Mrs. Hattie shared some encouraging words, which made Mary Jo realize how hard it is going to be for her little group not to have their friend. Pushing her plate back, she began to lose her appetite. The pungent scent of the food had lost its favor and her taste buds had gone sour. Mary Jo said, "Oh! Yes ma'am mama, Billy Ray is a pest at times, and he bothers me, but in a good kind of way. You understand what I'm trying to say? Huh Mama?" Mary Jo was trying to put into words how she felt about Billy Ray.

However, Mrs. Hattie feeling what Mary Jo is going through right at that moment said, "Baby, I's had friends like dat, but I's still love dem, Uh Hun!" Mary Jo half-heartedly laughed as she got up from the table and walked over to the scrap bucket. She scraped the left-over food for the chickens into the bucket. Mrs. Hattie took her plate and said, "Scram. Goes and find yore buddies." Mary Jo quickly went out onto the porch to wait on the steps. She looked up at the sky and thought, *if it stays like this all day, we can go swimming. I'm going to suggest this to Billy Ray when he comes over. It's been a while since we all have even thought about going swimming.*

She began to laugh as if someone was telling her something funny. Mary Jo was inspired as she got up from the steps talking out loud "look here, Billy Ray Sims. We should all go swimming. Do you hear me?"

At that moment Billy Ray said, "That's a good idea Mary Jo." Somewhat embarrassed, she cleared her throat as she did not realize that Billy Ray and B. J. were there.

CHAPTER II
WHAT IS GOING ON?

It is really getting hot now and the day is just starting. Billy Ray suggested taking the short cut down through the alley. B. J. knew that was a good idea and they could get there faster. He quickly agreed with Billy Ray, however, Mary Jo let her opinion be known. Mary Jo did not like going through the alley because the trees had big old, green worms dropping off of them. She knew there would be all types of creatures in that alley. This is definitely not the plan for her. "How dare the boys suggest such a thing like that? Me? Mary Jo, go through the alley again?" She was not moving from that spot.

"Oh shucks! Mary Jo," B. J. said. "I promise I won't play with any insects or bugs, O.K.?" As he looked at her with pleading eyes. Mary Jo popped those lips of hers and thought, *these boys better not be trying to tease me. Huh! They know I do not play.*

"Well!" Mary Jo said as she continued popping her lips as if she was eating something good. "I will go with y'all through the alley o.k." The boys were happy that she did not get into one of those debates with them. This looked like it was going to be a good day for the gang. Mary Jo felt peaceful as she looked up at the blue sky and thought about the summer and the good times they had.

Suddenly, B. J., of all people, stopped and said, "Hey gang! Let's go and see if Mr. Joe's plums are ripe yet." B. J. was always the first one to try to stop them from eating all those cherries.

"How dare he now suggest that we go checkout the plums. After all the toiling and pain I had to go through. They were not around to help me pull not one weed. Now the boy is talking about checking out the plum tree." This did not sit well with Mary Joe, after all she'd been through. Never in this life will she touch or eat off of any more trees.

"Ah!" Billy Ray said, as he boldly looked at Mary Jo with a question. "Are you chicken?" Immediately Billy Ray stopped and realized what he had asked Mary Jo. He was getting ready to have this girl talking about what happened. Her dirty hand and the darkness covered her. They would never get to where they were going now. Billy Ray was defeated now, as he stood there waiting for the big tongue-lashing.

He hit his head and looked at B.J. for some help. However, at once, this raging girl shouted, "You just take that back. I do more things than you scary boys do. You did not have to pull weeds until your fingernails looked like dirt, and the sun went down, and darkness was around you like a wet blanket."

"Oh, come on Mary Jo. Why do you always try to act like you're a movie star? That is so stale what you just quoted." Billy Ray said.

"You do not know what you are talking about Billy Ray, so just hush" Mary Jo said in a rage as she swayed from side to side. "You boys think you're so smart, but y'all do not know nothing."

Getting a word in finally, B. J. said, "Look!" as he pointed his finger in her face. "All I did was ask if y'all want to go? I did not intend for this to be a big discussion or the start of another war."

"Well!" Mary Jo said, huffing and puffing like she had just run a race. "I am not going, so stop asking me, B. J." He was still convinced that he could get Mary Jo to go. B. J. suggested they ask Mr. Joe this time. Knowing this was a good way to get Mary Jo to go alone.

B.J., with his big eyes, pleaded with Mary Jo, hoping she would go. This was a girl that did not like being pushed into doing anything that she did not come up with. However, she let the boys know she would think about it. She continued to lay down the rules and what she expected the boys to do. Immediately, B. J. pulled Billy Ray to the other side of the alley and said, "You got her started, now you need to stop her."

Billy Ray laughed as he went to do his fiendish act. He walked over to where Mary Jo was standing as she wondered what they had talked about for so long. The boys knew that this time of the year the trees in the alleyway had green caterpillars on them. These little creatures would fall out of the trees onto the ground. Billy Ray looked down and saw one crawling near Mary Jo's foot. Looking as if he was very concerned, he said softly "Mary Jo what is that near your foot?"

She looked down and the green, crawly thing was on top of her sandals. She let out a loud screech and stood there frozen in her tracks. Being very sensitive she said, "Oh, please Billy Ray get it off, kill it."

B. J. was going to play with her until he saw how afraid she was. He gently picked the caterpillar off her sandal and stuck it on a tree. She took off running as if a bear was after her. Billy Ray asked, "B. J., how come Mary Jo can go alley hunting and cannot stand the thing in the alley, huh?"

B. J. and Bill Ray know that this girl is impossible. Billy Ray lets out a slow "huh."

B.J. said "Mrs. Hattie ought to be glad she does not have any more children like her."

Billy Ray, laughing, said, "Boy you are so right. She is impossible."

For the most part, the boys needed to catch up with Mary Jo. The challenge is on now. B. J. and Billy Ray in a race to see who would be able to catch her. B. J., counting, said "On your mark, get set, go."

The two boys took off running. What a sight to see! They ran with their entire might, side by side however, Billy Ray sweating and huffing, trying to get his breath. He had really lost it during the summer months and should start running more often. Billy Ray looked down the street and saw Mary Jo running like a thoroughbred. She was gracefully placing her feet on the hard sidewalk. A soft breeze was blowing her two braids across her face as she enjoyed the run. She looked free and spirited.

"Hey!" B. J. shouted. "Wait up, Mary Jo." She turned and slowed down for B. J. to catch up. Trying to catch his breath, he humbly told Mary Jo how sorry he acted. Would she forgive him? B. J. confesses that it was his idea to get Billy Ray to scare her. The boys just wanted her to stop talking so much.

"Well!" Mary Jo said intently. "You boys are always playing tricks on us girls. You all act as if you are wild animals sometimes, B.J."

"Oh shucks, we did not," he said, as he hit the palm of his hand as if to prove what he said. "We meant no harm by it Mary Jo. You're just too scary to be so smart like you are." B. J. really opened up a can of worms by making that statement. This was all Mary Jo needed to get her point over. She really hit the nail on the head. She told the boys about the dumb things they do to girls as she put her hand on her bony hip. She made the boys see that what they did to her did not have anything to do with being smart.

"God just made girls that way!" she sharply replied. Mary Jo decided there was no point in her trying to make the boys understand her. She threw up her hands and concluded, "Boys do not know how to treat girls."

B. J. let out a pitiful, "Yeah, I guess we do not know how. But if we stay around you all we will learn, huh?"

Mary Jo looked at him and refused to waste anymore of her time. "Boys are too brainwashed to figure out girls." The boys apologized and Mary Jo accepted and gave them a group hug.

CHAPTER III
MARY JO AND HER OLD TRICKS

In the meantime, Mary Jo thought that she should tell B. J. what girls do not like. She made a big point hitting her hand as she told B. J. "We do not like snails, worms, crawling things, water bugs, June bugs, black bugs, flies, wasps, bees, or slimy snakes. O.k.? Now you know what girls do not like. Therefore, the next time you and your friend flyboy want to play tricks on me or the girls, do not do it."

Billy Ray quickly approached Mary Jo and politely told her he did not mean to scare her. Mary Jo could not believe these boys. She had a funny suspicion that they were up to something. However, for right now, she was enjoying the attention the boys were showering on her.

She Immediately sat on the curb. Stretching and rubbing her legs, she said, "Billy Ray and B. J. why don't y'all go get the twins, I'm tired." The boys were happy to get back on the good side of Mary Jo. They let her know they would be right back.

"Just sit there and rest," the boys happily told her. The boys act as if Mary Jo had given them a gift, as they head down the block. While walking, it suddenly hit them. Mary Jo is always tired and wants to stay back while they go and get the twins. Fiercely pounding his fist in his hand, Billy Ray angrily said, "This is the third time that she has fooled us into going to get the twins." B. J. nodded his head and hit his hand, as he agreed with Billy Ray. Needless to say, the boys continued down the block and noticed the twins patiently waiting for them.

For the most part, Mary Jo decided to sit at the curb and wait for the gang. She started to think about Billy Ray and how all of them got together this summer. It was a special summer, the best one yet, because they found each other after the twin's birthday party.

Wow! Mary Jo thought. That was the beginning of the joy of those summer days. Each adventure that the little gang created, the next adventure was sure to be more exciting. While sitting there, Mary Jo squinted her eyes and wiped the sweat with the end of her t-shirt. She laughed out-loud at some of the crazy things the gang did during the hot, muggy days. She had to admit that Billy Ray would be terribly missed. She thought she would never tell him that though.

Flyboy would never understand, as she laughed again. Still sitting on the curb, Mary Jo felt somewhat bad about making the boys go get the twins again. She was not all that tried. She was up to her old tricks, getting the boys to do what she wanted them to do.

Suddenly, Mary Jo realized that someone might be watching her as she sat at the curb. The people in this town would think that the sun had gotten to her. After all, she was sitting on a curb laughing out loud, and no one was with her. Like a flash, she quickly got up and dusted her shorts off. Standing there, she continued to act as if she was looking at something that got her attention. She thought, *wow, what a poor kid has to go through so grown- ups do not think you are crazy.*

At that moment, she looked down the street again to see if the twins and the boys were coming. Through the heat waves coming off the street, she could see four figures running up the block. The twins and the boys were waving their hands.

Phew! Mary Jo thought *it is too hot out here*, while still standing on the curb. The twins approached Mary Jo, jumping up and down. They were so happy to see her. Mary Jo was glad to see them too. They each hugged and gave their greetings. The girls wanted to know how each other had been doing.

"Oh, good Mary Jo", the twins said. "We missed playing with you." They seemed to say the words in the same breath. "What are we going to do today?"

Mary Jo replied, "Billy Ray would like to go swimming. Is that alright with you girls?" The twins quickly pulled their t-shirts up and showed Mary Jo their swimsuits. If Billy Ray did not want to go swimming, they would be walking around with those sweaty suits on all day. The twins solemnly said to Mary Jo that they were not going to keep talking and asking questions. She immediately nodded her head in agreement. The twins are acting like mockingbirds again, nodding *yes, yes*. They each pulled up their shirts again and showed Mary Jo their swimsuits on. They figured that was a smart thing to do just in case they would go swimming. Mary Jo could not believe the twins repeating what they had just said.

In the meantime, Billy Ray was trying to act like a cowboy. He had his lips turned up, talking out of the corner of his mouth saying, "Because I kind of like to swim all day."

"Twins, I'd like to go by Mr. Joe's and get some plums too, o .k?" The twins looked over at Mary Jo, still not giving Billy Ray an answer, but acting in their usual way, jumping up and down laughing. He could see how excited the twins were about going; however, this did not sit too well with their leader.

"Whoa! Wait just a minute gang," she began, as she beat the palm of her hand with her fist to let them know. "You, all did not," as she held up one finger, "have to pull weeds until the sun stopped shining." Two fingers went up as she showed them her hands. They were so dirty; you could not see her nails. "And three", as three little fingers went up, "you did not have nobody to talk to."

The twins, looking confused, did not know what Mary Jo was saying. They wondered when the sun ever went down over the horizon. They realized they missed a whole lot when they went on vacation. Shirley whispered to Sandy that they would not do any of their usual questioning, but had a puzzling look on their quiet little faces. Mary Jo sensed that the twins were not going to understand the way she was talking. She thought it was useless to try and change the subject.

"Gosh lee!" B. J. whispered to Billy Ray. "I thought we were going to have to hear her tell that story over again, huh?"

Billy Ray laughed and said, "Me too B. J., me too."

Mary Jo knew the boys were talking about her. She just rolled her eyes and let them have their fun. Quickly, Mary Jo said, "Come on gang it's getting late, and we have a lot planned for today."

The little gang hurried down to Clay Hill Creek to swim. As they got closer to the creek, Mary Jo thought it would be a good time to give her speech. After all, she could speak well, and the gang needed to hear her.

"Billy Ray Sims" echoed through the air as she said very sternly, moving closer to him. Then her speech began, "The gang is going to miss you terribly. You are the only Billy Ray on this earth and that's how the Lord wanted it to be. Ok Billy Ray?" He nodded his head and was wondering what in the world she was talking about. She continued, "We will", as she pointed her finger, "certainly be looking for another boy to take your place. It has been fun having you here with us this summer. We are going to miss swimming, the playhouse we built, the alley hunt and dinner my mama would make. Oh, let's not forget the twins' birthday party, the country fair, the movies, and most of all, the black hawk cherry tree happenings."

The twins, Billy Ray and B. J., were staring at Mary Joby this time and thinking, *Yeah, the sun has definitely gotten to her.*

Billy Ray's eyes were clouding up. He quietly talked about the good times they have had this summer. He knew it would soon be over for him. He sadly thanked the gang. Most of all, their great leader Mary Jo, for coming up with such great activities for them to do.

Mary Jo was surprised he could talk so well. She was dumbfounded as he continued to tell them goodbye. "Finally," he said, "I do not want to take the fun out of today so let's enjoy it, O.K.?"

On the other hand, the twins did not say a word, as they wondered why the Lord did not make two of Billy Ray. If he was, a twin could stay down here with them and the other one could go with his mama and daddy. For the most part, like a mothering hen, Mary Jo got everybody back to thinking about going swimming. It was not time to worry about Billy Ray's departure just yet. They still have several days left to have fun. The little gang yelled, "Yeah, yeah we are going to have some fun today." Billy Ray told the gang they still had six days left before he would leave. Everybody yelled "Yeah!" as loud as they could.

The gang reached the creek and noticed that it was dammed up. They each got ready to jump in the cold water. The twins were smart, as they had their swimsuits under their clothes. They had on matching, colorful swimsuits. The boys jumped into the water with some cut-off pants on. However, Mary Jo had on a black, sleek suit that had no curves and a flower that graced her waistline. "Is everybody ready?" Billy Ray shouted out as he came up out of the water again.

The twins were about to go in, when Mary Jo said, "We need to go over the rules first."

"What rules?" B. J. said, as he came up to the bank. "No dunking the girls or throwing water on us. We will get into the water when we get ready."

"Aar, rah," Billy Ray said, making fun of Mary Jo being chicken, as he got into the water. He teased Mary Jo about her not being able to swim.

CHAPTER IV
THE MOVE THAT SHOCKED THE GROUP

B.J. climbed up on a tree limb and did a belly flop into the water. The water splashed on Mary Jo. But she did not say anything. She just watched the twins, as they jumped into the cold water. "Oh! Oh!" she said, putting her toe in the water wanting to get in. She just could not bear jumping into that cold water. She figured the twins, and the boys must be hot-blooded. She thought, *I guess I am chicken,* as she looked at the gang enjoying themselves and all the fun she was missing. Mary Jo tried to get in several times but backed up from the water. The sun was hot, as it beamed down through the tree limbs. The water probably would feel good right now. Billy Ray decided to entertain the twins by doing his crazy dive. The twins looked at Billy Ray as he put his hands up and jumped feet first in the water.

Billy Ray, feeling a little embarrassed, wiped the water off his face and said, "My belly ain't hurting like B.J's is either." He took the opportunity to tell Mary Jo, "You not even in the water, scaredy cat."

Mary Jo, trying to please everyone, put her foot in the water but said, "Ooh-ooh that's too cold."

"Ah shucks Mary Jo. Everybody is having fun but you. Come on," Billy Ray said.

Mary Jo was not getting her little body wet. She stuck her toes in the water and quickly drew them back. Mary Jo could hear the gang tell her, "The only way you are going to get used to the water is to jump in." Miss Star let the little gang know she'd get in when she was ready and sat back down on the bank.

Mary Jo sat on the bank thinking; *I am going to give this gang a surprise of their lives. Let me get my nerves up. I need to stop thinking about how cold the water is. If I count one, two, three and jump in, I won't feel the chilly water. Yeah, that is what I am going to do.* She was proud of herself, as she stood up and acted as if she was going to jump in.

The twins got out of the water and said, "Mary Jo, is this what you came down here for? You are just standing on the bank and watching us swim?" Mary Jo started to answer the twins but decided not to get them started. She chose to give the twins one of her evil eye looks.

Indeed, you can bet the twins really got her silent message and jumped back in the water. "Huh!" She thought. "Finally, I can use the silent act on the twins. It's good to know that the evil-eye works." She laughed and continued thinking about how she was going to get into the cold water. Once she gets her body to cooperate with her mind, the gang is going to get the shock of their lives. Mary Jo has a big secret that she is waiting to spring it on the gang. Out of all the surprises that she has come up with, this one will take the cake. She knows the gang will be standing with their mouths open wide enough to drive a truck into it.

Mary Jo was feeling good about herself just knowing what was in store for the gang. She wrapped her arms around herself and thought about what she had accomplished without the gang. She was so pleased with herself. The hard work has paid off and now she's happy she can swim. In that moment of bliss, Mary Jo was standing on the bank as if she was the star swimmer of the day. Her eyes closed as she put her hands up over her head. The twins stared at her and thought she was acting as if she was getting ready to be baptized or something. Shirley looked over at Sandy to see if she noticed. With their round, brown eyes, the twins could not believe that this girl hadn't opened her eyes yet.

"How is she going to see the water with her eyes closed, Shirley?" Sandy asked, looking confused. Nevertheless, Miss Drama queen was about to give the little gang the shock of their little lives. Mary Jo has finally made up her mind to forget how cold the water is. She decided not to look at the water, but just dive in. She could feel the warm sun rays shining on her face. She held her breath, as she prepared herself to hit the cold water.

In the meantime, the boys had taken notice of Mary Jo standing on the bank with her eyes closed. Billy Ray was wondering why she had her eyes closed and her hands over her head. If she was getting into the water, it did not take all of that. "Who does she think she is?" Billy Ray thought, "Esther Williams?" He had to laugh for even thinking like that.

On the other hand, B. J. was not wasting his time trying to see what Mary Jo was up to. He came down to the creek to swim and that is what he was doing. He was acting like a motorboat. He was blowing bubbles with his mouth and kicking his feet like a motor. The twins were still looking up at Mary Jo, wanting to know what was going on with her. She was still standing on the bank with her eyes closed and her hands over her head. The twins knew, from their previous experience, that this girl could come up with some strange things and started to wonder if she was having one of those sun problems that the grown-ups talked about.

Nevertheless, all at once, the twins saw Mary Jo dive into the water like a diving bird. She glided smoothly through the water and came up, only to take some breath. Both of the twins grasped at the same time. They quickly put their hands over their mouths in disbelief. They were overcome with shock as they stood up in the water, looking at Mary Jo.

By this time the boys saw what Mary Jo had done. She was in the water swimming like a fish and acting like that great movie star, Esther Williams. She looked as if she enjoyed swimming. Her strokes were perfect, as she gracefully glided across the water. The boys were dumbfounded. They could not believe what they were seeing. Mary Jo was swimming through the water as if she had been swimming for a long time.

The boys got out of the water to watch in awe. They were astonished at what their eyes were beholding. Mary Jo knew they were watching her. She really put on a show, as she swam around in the water. She swam back to the bank like a beautiful swan. The 'ugly duck' was not there anymore and now the gang can stop teasing her.

Mary Jo quickly got out of the water and wiped her face. She was so happy that she could finally show the gang she could swim. The twins were hurrying to get out of the water. They wanted to find out who taught her how to swim. They proudly gathered around her like she was a movie star. "When did you learn how to swim?" the boys excitedly asked, while looking embarrassed at making fun of her earlier.

"Well!" Mary Jo said, "while the twins were gone, and you and Billy Ray did not come around that much. I came down here and practiced every other day."

"Wow!" Billy Ray said, "you can almost swim better than all of us, Mary Jo." She could outswim the whole gang now and she showed them everything she knew about swimming. Mary Jo just went along with Billy Ray's comment.

"Oh really?" She said as she climbed out of the water and sat on the bank. They were amazed at how well she could use her arms. She really surprised them when she stayed under the water for a while. B. J. stared and did not ask her any questions. The twins had to know where Mary Jo learned to swim so well. The never-ending questions.

CHAPTER V
THE GANG IN DISBELIEF

The twins just did not want to believe that this girl could swim so well. It was amazing that Mary Jo knew how to swim, and they had not taught her. This was too much for the twins to comprehend. Mary Jo could see the frustration on the twins' faces. They knew Mary Jo was the smart one in the gang, however, when it came to swimming, she did not know anything.

Mary Jo laughed at the twins and their many questions. She told them she didn't have anyone to play with while they were gone so, when she would get lonely or bored, she'd go down to the creek and swim. "Yes, the water was cold, but I would get in anyway," she said.

Mary Jo did not realize she had opened a can of worms because the twins jumped right on what she said. They were like little birds with their mouths wide open waiting to eat. The twins asked Mary Jo, "Why did it take you so long to get into the water, huh? You could swim the whole time you were standing on that bank. What was with your hands over your head huh?"

Billy Ray, Mary Jo, and B. J. could not believe what they were hearing. These two little spoiled brats have the nerve to be mad because Mary Jo can swim. Billy Ray went over to the twins and explained to them that it was alright.

"It's just amazing, Mary Jo, what you have accomplished," the twins said. Mary Jo just couldn't believe the twins using one of their spelling words.

Mary Jo, hitting her forehead, said "Those little stinkers remembered such a big word and used the word in its proper place."

"Practice!" Mary Jo walked over to where the twins were standing. She gently put her arms around them like little children and repeated, "Practice." The boys ran and jumped into the water waving for everyone to join. They all happily jumped back into the cold water. They played until their skin was wrinkled. Mary Jo was having the time of her life. She could finally enjoy the water like the others.

Mary Jo decided to go along with the gang and ask Mr. Joe if they could have some plums. The gang yelled out, "All right, Mary Jo, we are so glad you changed your mind." Mr.

Joe's plums were just right for picking. He gladly allowed the gang to pick some plums for his fruit stand, which was located near the highway.

The gang did not waste any time climbing into the plum trees. The trees were full of those purple plums and this little gang did not have any problems picking them. They also enjoyed loading up their pockets with plums to eat on the way home. The little gang was not concerned about getting sick this time. The plums were much bigger than the cherries, so the gang would not be able to load their stomachs up as much.

They picked five baskets of plums for Mr. Joe to sell at his fruit stand. He thanked them and let them know they could come back and pick plums any time they wanted. They were happy they asked before getting into Mr. Joe's plums this time.

"Wow!" Billy Ray said. "This was a great day, gang. One I will forever remember." On the way home, the gang told Mary Jo how much they enjoyed the summer. They were still looking forward to more of her adventures. The sun slowly went down, as the gang went their separate ways for the evening.

Mary Jo was glad the boys saw the twins home. She felt good knowing that she made the last couple of days enjoyable for Billy Ray. She thought to herself, *this is just the beginning*. Mary Jo's little heart had not been this happy in a while. Maybe Billy Ray should have left earlier.

"Wow! I guess we would have been too tired to do anything by now," she sighed. The things we do and create just make our lives worth living; especially, the fresh fruits that all of the neighbors seem to have in their yards. The kids would get in trouble eating the fruit before their time. After being warned about how it would make their little stomach hurt, they would have the flux. This was all about learning the things you should do and not do.

The well-laid plans that Mary Jo would come up with made their summer so much fun. That special pleasure that shined through the gang's eyes was a joy in discovering the world around them. Mary Jo looked up at the evening sky and said, "What a day this has been for our little group. They learned it was better to ask than to assume." Mary Jo thought that was why her mama always laid down rules. The rules did not seem important at first, but Mary Jo is slowly realizing that her mama is smart and some of that is rubbing off on her. She had to laugh as she thought to herself that *grown-ups are strange at times.*

While nearing her home, Mary Jo thought about what they could do next. The weekend was coming up and she needed a plan, however, she still had time. This day proved to be special because she finally could show she knew how to swim.

"What a day" she said, as she jumped up, remembering how the twins reacted to her knowing how to swim. Shirley and Sandy were a little perturbed because they did not get the opportunity to teach Mary Jo to swim. Most of all, how surprised Billy Ray and B. J. were when they saw how she took off swimming like a fish. Earlier, the boys were calling her chicken and scaredy cat, but they had to take it all back. She showed the gang that she could outswim all of them. Throwing up her hands, Mary Jo was happy about the day's events, as it turned out to be a learning lesson for the gang. They now know the true meaning of believing in themselves, asking before picking from fruit trees, and giving your friends a chance to join in activities.

CHAPTER VI
SUNDAY MORNING

Mary Jo smuggled up against her mama, as she listened to the soft rain spattering across the windowpane. She thought it was going to be one of those wet, boring Sundays. Mary Jo had plans for the gang to go to the blackberry patch today.

Putting her hand under her chin, she desperately needed her prayer answered. "You see Lord, I need it to stop raining. I have something special planned for the gang today and if it continues we won't be able to go." At this point, she could not even hear a pin falling to the floor. She perked up her ears and listened attentively, but to no avail. Then she said, "Lord did you hear me?" In a soft voice. "I cannot talk too loud because my mama is asleep, and I do not want to wake her."

Little did Mary Jo know the weather would be nice later on in the day. Mrs. Hattie began to stir, and Mary Jo eased herself back down in the bed. She thought, *If I do not breathe too loudly, maybe mama won't wake up. Then, we can stay in bed all day. It is raining and there is no use for us to get up now.*

However, Mary Jo's mama knew it was time for them to get up. Mrs. Hattie rose and stretched. "Mary Jo, baby, it's time to start getting ready for Sunday School" she said.

Quickly sitting up in the bed, Mary Jo exclaimed, "Mama, it's raining outside. Why do we have to go to Sunday School?"

Mrs. Hattie, getting out of bed, said, "Cause, Mary Jo, this is de Lord's Day. Now get yoes self-up. Wes going to church dis morning child."

Mary Jo shrugged her shoulders and said, "Yes ma'am, mama." She slowly made up the bed and sat in the chair near the night table.

In the meantime, Mrs. Hattie was busy getting Mary's clothes ready. She picked out a nice Sunday-best dress, her slip, socks, and some underwear. Then she said, "Mary Jo go look in de closet for yore patent leather shoes. Oh! Do not forget yore raincoat, it's really raining out there."

Mumbling, Mary Jo found her shoes in the closet and that dreadful raincoat. Then, she went over and pressed her face on the cool, moist windowpane and stared at the rain. She said under her breath, "Maybe we can go to the blackberry patch tomorrow. I just hope mama doesn't start that darn (oops) old canning again." She quickly looked around, almost getting a crook in her neck, to see what her mama was doing. She was still in the bathroom. "Whew!" Mary Jo said, "Mama did not hear me."

Still looking out at the rain, Mary Jo had a pep talk with herself. She thought, *girl, you need to stop hanging around them boys. They are making you say "darn" too much and one of these days your mama is going to hear you. And you know what that will get you huh?* Mary Jo laughed as she thought about her mama's garden and the many weeds she had to pull up.

For the most part, that little talk did not put a damper on the rain. It was raining as if it was coming out of a faucet. Every now and then, it would thunder and lightning. "Gosh! Look at all that rain", Mary Jo said. "Mama talking about going to Sunday school. Sometimes I think mama is not thinking right. She should stay out of that garden because the sun is frying her brain." Still feeling her mama should not go out in this kind of weather, Mary Jo began to think of some more things that the gang could do, although most people would just stay home.

At that moment, a big streak of lightning flashed across the sky. The lightning frightened Mary Jo, so she ran over to the bed and cried, "Oh please! Forget what I said about my mama's brain being fried. I am not worried about a little rain. B. J. loves the rain and flyboy likes it too. If it stops raining a little then, we will go to the blackberry patch anyway."

Mary Jo calmly sat on the bed and swung her legs against the bed railing. She thought about Billy Ray leaving in six days. She knew it was not going to be the same without him. Indeed, the boy was weird and at times, however, the gang was going to miss him.

In the meantime, Mrs. Hattie called out "Mary Jo, whose dat yocs talking too?" Mary Jo had to answer her mama and fast. She did not want her mama to know that she was thinking her brain must be fried from being in that garden of hers. Mary Jo did not want her mama to come back into the room. She hurried to the bathroom to get dressed. Then, Mary Jo let her mama know she was just playing and singing. Mrs. Hattie told Mary Jo to hurry up and get dressed. She was going to fix her a little breakfast. Mary Jo had to laugh because her mama does not know how to cook a little breakfast.

Her mama went to the kitchen to start breakfast. She walked over to the stove and poked around in the coals. Mr. Bill banked the fire the night before, so that she could have a fire in the morning. Beside the stove was a wood box where Mrs. Hattie took out some kindling wood to add to the fire. She noticed that it would not take long before the fire would be hot enough to start cooking.

Mary Jo took her time getting dressed. She looked in the mirror while still trying to figure out why her mama wanted to go out in the rain. "Ugh!" she grunted, as she poked out her lips, thinking about that yellow raincoat her mama wanted her to wear. "That old coat makes me look like a big sunflower," she said, as she threw her hands up in disgust.

CHAPTER VII
THE SWEET AROMA

Oftentimes, Mr. Bill would make the coffee early and leave it on the back of the stove. The aroma from the coffee would stimulate Mrs. Hattie's taste buds. She picked up her favorite cup from the little shelf and poured herself a cup of coffee. Her nose took in the scent as she said, "Hum, hum, hum! Dis coffee tastes as good as it smells." Sipping the coffee, she suddenly realized that it was getting late. She called for Mary Jo to come to breakfast.

As usual, Mary Jo jumped down two steps at a time. She knew her mama would tell her to walk down the stairs like a young lady. She had a hardy attitude, as she went into the kitchen and flopped down at the table. Mrs. Hattie had the country breakfast smell filling the air in the kitchen.

The pungent smell of a good breakfast engulfed her senses and Mary Jo's attitude quickly disappeared. She thought, *forget the rain. I'm hungry.* A smile crossed her face, as her mom gave her a plate. Right away, she began to pile the food in her mouth, as if she was starving. She was acting as if she was not going to get another meal.

Mrs. Hattie noticed Mary Jo and told her "Slow down, dat food is not going nowhere but in your mouth." Mary Jo, smiling, continued putting a piece of ham in her mouth. Mrs. Hattie laughed and sipped her coffee. The big clock on the wall was ticking so loud that her mama noticed time and realized it was time to go.

"Oh! "My goodness" Mrs. Hattie said, "Childe yoes better hurry up and finish up. It's almost time for Sunday school." Mary Jo finished and wiped her mouth with the back of her hand. Mrs. Hattie gave Mary Jo the look. She could hear those words without her mama opening up her mouth. "Now yoes know better than dat Mary Jo. Git up and git yoeself a cup towel" Her mama would say. "Wipe yore hands and mouth on it. Yoe noes I taught yoes better than dat Mary Jo."

"Yes ma'am, mama!" Mary Jo said, as she got a cup towel off of the little table sitting up by the window. Mary Jo quickly picked up the nice, starched cup towel with *Sunday* embroidered on it with different colors of thread. Surprised at the fact that it was not raining anymore, she thought maybe the gang would be able to go to the blackberry patch after all.

"Huh?" Mary Jo said, my prayer is answered. She let out praises of joy. "Oh! Thank you, thank you, thank you!" she shouted.

Her mama was wondering why Mary Jo was talking to herself and acting strange. "What is yoe doing, Mary Jo?" Mrs. Hattie asked. Mary Jo acted like she did not hear her mama, but Mrs. Hattie was wise to Mary Jo, ignoring her. Mrs. Hattie continued to clean the table off. Mrs. Hattie just gave Miss Mary Jo the look again.

This helped Mary Jo come up with a good answer. "The gang is going to the blackberry patch. Ah, maybe I could bring some blackberries back and you can make one of those blackberry cobblers, huh mama?"

"We see how you act in church service today. Yoe noes y'all be acting out when grown folks get busy with the Lord's business. I's see y'all laughing and talking loud cause yoe think no one is looking at y'all huh, yoe don't fool me." Her mama said in response.

Mary Jo, trying to get on the good side of her mama said, "I am an angel, and you know I do not act like those other children, laughing and talking all the time." Mrs. Hattie almost choked, as she drank her last drop of coffee.

Laughing, her mama said, "Baby yoe an angel only when yoes sleeping." Mary quickly finished cleaning the table off and went upstairs to get the dreaded raincoat from her closet floor. In the meantime, Mrs. Hattie walked down the hallway to get her purse, hat and coat out of the closet. She carefully put on a hat that Mary Jo found one day. She smiled as she looked in the hallway mirror, admiring the hat as she put it to one side. Being a little conceited, Mrs. Hattie said, "This is shore enough a pretty hat and I shore can wear it too." It was a beautiful hat. The hat had spring flowers and a veil that hung just below the bridge of her nose. Her ebony skin and light brown eyes brought out the color in the feathers. She laughed as she thought about some of the women at church refusing to look her way.

In the meantime, Mary Jo was coming down the stairs like a lady, only because her mama was standing in the hallway. She was feeling as if it was not going to be a good day, all because of that yellow raincoat. She drugged it down each step that she took. It's too wet, cold, and dreary outside. She thought, *even the fish don't like it today and they live in water.*

Mary Jo could not seem to get it together and thought she should have pretended to be sick to stay in bed. Everything was wrong. In other words, Mary Jo was feeling like this because she thought she was the smartest one in her Sunday class. The teacher would let her read the Bible stories because she always read with expression. The class would sit perfectly still, as their little ears listened to every word. She already knew the story about Mary and Joseph. Nevertheless, that did not matter to Mrs. Hattie. Mary Jo was going to Sunday School and that was that. As usual, Mary Jo got near the last steps and refused to walk down them. She just jumped to the floor. Her mama did not say a word to her. Instead, she just gave her the look again. Mary Jo knew that look would be her last one today. Mary Jo stopped and thought that it was a good thing that children did not die from the looks that grown-ups gave them. It would just be a world full of old people. She'd better get it together or suffer the consequences, which without a doubt, was not going to happen today. The gang needed to go to the blackberry patch, so she needed to be good at Sunday school and church. Whatever was in the look, it worked. Most children would get themselves together and behave.

Mrs. Hattie grabbed an umbrella from the stand near the door and motioned for Mary Jo to come on. She opened the door and stepped out onto the porch letting the umbrella up. Following behind her mama, Mary Jo put the yellow raincoat on and said, "Ugh! Just look at this coat, mama." With a questionable look on her face, Mary Jo asked, "Who decided a raincoat has to be yellow? It is not cute. I look like a sunflower."

Knowing that Mary Jo does not like the raincoat, her mama kindly said, "Little girl yoes my sunflower," and busted out with a hearty laugh. Mrs. Hattie gained her composure and told her that the raincoat would keep her dry. "Now, come for wes be late to Sunday school."

CHAPTER VIII
A MOST NEEDED RIDE

Even though the sun was trying to shine, there were big clouds in the sky. Knowing this weather, it might start raining at any time. Mrs. Hattie noticed the change in the weather too and told Mary Jo to come on before it started to rain again. This is all Mary Jo needed; to be outside in a yellow raincoat. The kids would have a good time laughing about not getting wet with this thing on. "We will get wet when it rains, if I do not have this old darn (oops)," as she did not say the word out loud. *Mary Jo, if you do not stop saying that word, you are going to get into trouble,'* she thought. *I have better things to do than get caught using words I am not supposed to say.*

Mrs. Hattie and Mary Jo were hurrying down the street on their way to church. At that moment, they spotted Mrs. Johnson driving down the street. Mrs. Hattie rushed over to the curb, waving her hand. Mrs. Johnson quickly pulled over and said, "Come, Mrs. Hattie, get in. We are going your way.

This was all Mrs. Hattie needed, as she said, "Glory Be! Thank you, Mrs. Johnson, for stopping for us. We did not want to be out in this weather and get rained on. Thank you again." Hurrying to get in, Mary Jo sat in the backseat with the twins and Mabel. The twins were happy that Mary Jo was going to Sunday school with them.

Shirley was at it again asking, "What is the gang doing today?" Looking over at Mabel, she told the twins they could talk later. The twins both nodded their heads simultaneously.

In the meantime, Mrs. Johnson and Mrs. Hattie were having a good time, talking about that hat. Mrs. Johnson smiled and said, "Mrs. Hattie, girl, you shore wearing that hat. You got it cocked at the right side of your head like you've come out of King's Major Department store downtown. Honey you better tell the truth," as she let out a big belly laugh. All that Mrs. Hattie could do was laugh at what Mrs. Johnson had said. She knew it was going to be a lot more said about that hat once she got to church. Mrs. Johnson was just giving her a prelude to what was really going to happen. The women at church are going to be so out done, that they'd probably look the other way. Not all of the women at church are like that, but there's always a few who just can't stand to see anyone else look better than them. After the conversation about the hat, the women talked about something else. Mrs. Johnson and Mrs. Hattie began discussing, "When Mrs. Jones going to stop having so many babies, money and the fact that the pastor needs a good woman, like Mrs. Hattie."

"Whoa!" she said. "Mrs. Johnson, that will never happen. Yoes noes the women at the church would move their membership. Now yoe noes dat would be something."

"Honey you shore knows what you are talking about, girl," Mrs. Johnson said, laughing.

Finally, they arrived at the church and noticed Sunday school was just getting out. Mary Jo and the twins were happy that Sunday school was over. They kind of enjoyed church services; especially if they could sit in the back. Mary Jo said, "Mama, may I take my raincoat off. It's not raining now."

Mrs. Hattie said, "Shore child and don't yoe be losing it, hean?" Mary Jo was so happy, as she hurriedly took the raincoat off. Mrs. Hattie politely reminded Mary Jo that she had a few more wears out of that coat.

Suddenly, Mary Jo saw the opportunity to ask her mama about sitting in the back seat. "Uh, uh, mama," she said. "May I sit in the back today?"

Her mama said, "Yeah and yoes noes how to behave, Mary Jo."

The twins were excited, as they asked their mama too. "Yes, girls and behave. You hear?" As usual, acting like mockingbirds, the twins nodded their heads yes.

Mrs. Hattie and Mrs. Johnson walked down the church aisle. They took the front row of seats in the choir stand and sat down. All eyes were on Mrs. Hattie and that hat. Some of the ladies smiled and some looked the other way. Mrs. Hattie carefully took the hat off, brushed her hair with her hand, and looked out and smiled. Mrs. Johnson also got herself situated. She put her purse by her chair and smiled. Mabel took a seat near the middle aisle so she could keep her eye on the kids.

In the meantime, Mary Jo and the twins stretched their little necks, trying to spot B. J. They giggled under their breath at the funny-looking hats the ladies were wearing. The twins said, "Mary Jo, look, look, at that hat. It's a lampshade." This really got the girls laughing as they tried to hold a straight face. At one point, the girls were laughing so hard that they had to moan.

Shirley, pleading, said, "Mary Jo, please stop talking about them hats. Our mama's are going to look back here and they will make us move to the front seats."

"Oh!" Mary Jo said, "I won't talk. Just look for B. J., O.K.?"

Shirley and Sandy sat on the edge of the pew and spotted B. J. near the front seat. "Yeah! Uh Hun! We see him, Mary Jo," they said. B. J. stirred around in his seat, looking for Mary Jo, but could not find her.

Then, his mama said, "Boy, if you do not stop squirming in that seat. I am going to take yoes outside." B. J. knew what that meant, a good tanning on his behind.

Sitting motionlessly, he thought, *I've got to come up with something before church.* He got an idea, as he gently tapped his mama on the shoulder. "Mudear!" B. J. whispered. "I've got to use it." His mama gave him the look and told him to hurry back.

CHAPTER IX
LOOKING FOR MARY JO

B. J. excused himself and walked down the middle aisle, looking from side to side trying to find Mary Jo. Meanwhile, Mary Jo was trying to find B. J., as well. She saw him and immediately waved her hand, motioning for him to come to the back pew. B. J. quickly hurried down the aisle to where Mary Jo and the twins were sitting. "Gosh lee! Mary Jo." B. J. said. "I've been looking for you all morning in Sunday school." B. J. did not arrive at Sunday school on time because he was fooling around at home. Nonetheless, he was glad that he found Mary Jo. He was ready to know what was going on today. He really did not have to ask Mary Jo because she wanted to tell him about going to the blackberry patch.

Mary Jo got herself together and said, "Let me see, uh, uh." She put her hand under her chin, as if she was really thinking. The twins were waiting impatiently for Mary Jo to tell B. J. what they had planned for today. Mary Jo continued to stand there, looking silly, so the twins decided they would tell him.

Sandy said, "Guess what B. J., we are going to the blackberry patch after church. Do you want to go?"

This was too much for Mary Jo and she was so out done that she said, "Well I was going to tell him Sandy."

B. J. said, "It's alright Mary Jo. That is a good plan, and I will ask Mudear if I can go." He headed back up the aisle and remembered he really had to go. He turned around before Murdear could see him and went out the door.

By this time, Mary Jo was really peed at the twins for stealing her glory. She wanted to play with B. J. a little and Sandy had to mess up the plan. In the meantime, Shirley stepped up and asked Miss Mary Jo, "Why didn't you just tell him that we were going to the blackberry patch. Huh?"

Feeling a little disgusted with the twins' smartness, Mary Jo said, "I was going to tell him. Sandy didn't give me a chance. She just babbled it out before I could say anything."

At the same time, the twins said, "Mary Jo, you look like you were daydreaming with your hand under your chin." Sensing that she could not out-talk the twins she agreed with them.

Still aware that they were in church, Mary Jo said, "Twins the service is getting ready to start. Y'all be quiet." The twins quietly sat back in their seats as the choir began to sing. Mary Jo was clapping her hands and shaking her head to the music. Mrs. Hattie was singing the solo and this really made her feel good.

Then, unexpectedly, Mary Jo said something funny and that got the twins laughing again. Mrs. Hattie looked back every now and then and Mary Jo pretended she was an angel. "We need to act right twins, and I hate being sneaky." Mary Jo said.

The twins shyly said "Alright, Mary Jo, we won't laugh anymore." They put on their innocent faces and tried to be quiet during the rest of the services.

Finally, the church service was over. All the children piled out of the church door as if they had been set free from detention. Some children were laughing, little boys were chasing the girls and the grown folk were visiting each other. The single women chose to swarm around the pastor like flies on a honeycomb. Mrs. Hattie and Mrs. Johnson shook their heads at the way those women were acting. "Un hum!" Mabel grunted, shaking her head in disbelief.

For the most part, B. J., Mary Jo, and the twins were not concerned with what the grown-ups were talking about or who was looking at the pastor. They were ready to go, and their parents continued to laugh and talk about things that were not important to them. Mary Jo was ready to go home to change her clothes. She knew they would have to go by to see if Billy Ray could go too.

The day is almost gone and here we stand doing nothing. Mary Jo said, "Sandy, please ask your mama if we can go." At this point, Mary Jo was feeling frustrated and very impatient. Mrs. Johnson looked over at the children and noticed how sad they looked. She knew it was time to head home. They all followed her to the car and quickly got in. Mabel, looking at the girls, said, "what's the hurry to git home huh? Yoe going to find some trouble to get into girls?" They did not say anything to Mabel. They simply shook their heads no.

Mrs. Hattie decided to tell Mabel what the children were up to. She told her that they had plans to go to the blackberry patch. Mrs. Johnson said, "That's why you all are being good hum the little stinkers." Mabel laughed and looked at the twins. She said "Yoes trying to be good huh! Playing on yore mama's feeling." The twins did not dare say anything to Mabel now because their mama might change her mind. In addition, Mary Jo knew not to say anything. She could not let Mabel's taunting bother them. She had a plan, and this little gang was going to be on their "p's" and "q's." Mary Jo knew how much time they would have if the twins hurried home and made a quick change. She leaned over and whispered to the twins to meet her at her house. The twins agreed to come over as soon as they changed their clothes.

"Oh, alright twins," Mary Jo said. "We can go by and get Billy Ray and go to the blackberry patch from there." This adventure would not include getting into trouble, as it is a big, open field that no one bothered to take care of. The twins could not wait until they got home. This was an exciting day. They were going to eat and pick sweet, juicy blackberries. In the meantime, Mrs. Johnson and Mrs. Hattie were talking. The girls wanted Mrs. Johnson to drive faster. The girls wished their moms would stop all their talking, as they were excited, and time was a wasting.

CHAPTER X
HOME AT LAST

Finally, without realizing it, they pulled up in front of Mrs. Hattie's house. She went out and thanked Mrs. Johnson for taking her and Mary Jo to and from church. While Mary Jo was getting out of the car, she noticed the dreaded yellow raincoat was nowhere to be found. "No!" Mary Jo cried from within. In the meantime, Mrs. Hattie was so busy talking to Mrs. Johnson that she didn't realize that Mary Jo did not have the raincoat.

Mary Jo quickly jumped out of the car, waving goodbye to the twins. She hurried up the steps to the porch and quickly opened the door. She took a deep breath and said, "That was a close call." She knew her mama would've asked her about that raincoat. Mary Jo could hear her call out for her to hang her clothes up. "Yes ma'am, mama," Mary Jo happily said. She quickly found some shorts and a shirt, then ran downstairs to wait on the twins. She thought she'd better wear her sandals today since the ground was still wet from the rain.

In the meantime, Mrs. Hattie was coming from the kitchen and wanted to know if Mary Jo would like a sandwich. She could feel her stomach at this time and quickly shook her head yes. Mrs. Hattie laughed and asked her why she was not saying anything. "Tom, the cat, got yore tongue?" She knew that was sure to get a response out of Mary Jo. Just the mention of that dumb cat would get Mary Jo started. Mrs. Hattie laughed and went back to the kitchen to make her a sandwich.

Following her mama into the kitchen, Mary Jo asked if she could have more of the country ham. Mrs. Hattie already had a feeling that Mary Jo would want a ham sandwich and a glass of her favorite drink, Kool-Aid. Mary Jo happily munched on her sandwich and drank her Kool-Aid. Suddenly, she could hear the twins calling her name. She immediately jumped up and ran to the front door. "Twins, how did you all get here so fast?" Mary Jo asked.

"Oh! Mabel took us in the car. Are you ready Mary Jo huh, huh," Sandy asked.

"Yeah! Just give me a minute, Sandy," Mary Jo said. She went back to the kitchen to tell her mama she was leaving. Of course, Mrs. Hattie had to lay the rules down for Mary Jo again and told her to behave herself. Mary Jo got the pail from under the sink and ran to the front door where the twins were waiting. She said, "let's go twins. We have to go by Billy Ray's house and get him. B. J. said he'd be waiting on the path."

The twins and Mary Jo went up the street to pick–up B.J. She knew the twins were preparing to ask her twenty questions again. Mary Jo decided not to get upset and she answered all their questions. The day turned out great and the girls were glad to be going on another adventure. Mary Jo thought this is what summer is all about: having fun with your friends. She put her hands up and laughed, as the twins wondered what was wrong with Mary Jo this time.

The sun was getting hotter as the girls approached the path. Through haze, they saw B.J. waving, as he yelled, "Come on slowpokes." Mary Jo and the twins started running to catch up with him. B.J. thought to himself, *boy this is going to be a great day.* He wanted to thank Mary Jo for such a great idea, however, his brain told him to leave it alone. He smiled and thought about those juicy, sweet black berries. In the meantime, Mary Jo let the gang know how hard it is for her to come up with different things for them to do.

Nevertheless, the twins were on their job and quickly responded to what Mary Jo said. "We did this same thing last year, Mary Jo and it's nothing that we have not done" the twins smartly said.

"Yeah! Twins, that is right," B.J. said. "We shore did do this last year, huh?" This really stirred Mary Jo up. "Well! So, what if we did?" Mary Jo asked angrily. "I noticed none of you could think of anything. Oomph!" The girl has fallen off her soapbox again. She was mad, mad and madder at the twins. She thought, "I did not think they could remember anything. Now, they are talking about what we did last year huh?" This was a little too much for Mary Jo to deal with. The weather alone was enough to make her run to the nearest creek. She decided to walk ahead of the twins so she would not have to talk to them.

Shirley softly whispered to Sandy, "Do you think Mary Jo is mad at us?"

Sandy looked sad as she told Shirley, "Indeed", Mary Jo was mad. We have to get back on the good side of Mary Jo." Coming up with an idea, Sandy said, "I know what we could do to make Mary Jo feel better."

Mary Jo turned around and noticed the twins in deep conversation. She thought, *what are the twins up to now?* She turned back around and continued walking by herself. The twins did not even see her, as they decided to say nice things about Mary Jo, like how much they enjoyed everything that she had planned for them. They turned to B. J. saying, "It is so nice of Mary Jo to plan all these good things for us to do huh?"

B. J. totally agreed with the twins and said, "That Mary Jo did a great job making sure we had a good time." They appreciated everything she had done for them throughout the summer. B. J. humbly said, "Gee Whiz! Mary Jo. I guess we have been a little selfish and not telling you thanks."

That did it. Mary Jo stopped and said casually, "Oh it's nothing, gang. I enjoyed doing it, but it is kinda hard trying to plan for the boys too."

The twins were trying to get on the good side of Mary Jo. They decided to join the cause with Mary Jo by telling B. J. "It's hard for us girls trying to plan things for you boys."

Mary Jo could not do anything but laugh and shake her head at the twins. The twins noticed Mary Jo laughing and knew that she had forgotten about being mad at them. All was well with the little gang as they continued down the road. While walking and feeling the heat of the day, Mary Jo decided to take her sandals off and walk in the soft mud. In the meantime, the twins were watching every move Mary Jo was making. Imitating everything Mary Jo was doing, the twins immediately sat down in the road and took off their sandals. Wiggling their toes, the twins started walking again. Mary Jo observed the little things the twins were doing like her. She was relieved that the annoying twins were not asking her twenty questions. *Huh!* She thought to herself. *Maybe the twins are learning something after all.*

The morning rain had cooled things down a little, however, the sun was slowly forcing its way through the fluffy, white clouds. B. J. could feel the humid air, as he took off his T-shirt. In spite of the thick air, he was enjoying the shade from the other side of the road. There was no shade where Mary Jo and the twins were walking. He figured it was good that they were across the road because the girls weren't able to bug him. This is why he wanted to hurry up and get Billy Ray. The boys needed each other because Mary Jo and the twins could be a handful at times.

Mary Jo always wanted the boys to kill every little bug or fly. Sticking out his flat, scary chest again, he said, "Huh! I like bugs and the good Lord said I could collect them." Oh, he was really feeling his worth now saying things about the good Lord. Suddenly, right in front of him, was a big, green frog sitting on a rock minding its business. B. J. immediately noticed the frog and a wave of joy came over him. What a surprise. The good Lord knew he loved his creatures. You could hear this boy yelling to the top of his voice, as if it was Christmas. "Boy oh boy!" B. J. said. "Look at that prize I just caught." This frog was a little bit smarter than B. J. figured. The slippery frog leaped out B. J.'s hand over into the tall grass. "Gee Whiz!" B. J. said, "I could have had a frog to take home." Feeling cheated, B. J. kicked in the dirt and threw up his hands. It was enough to make a kid go mad.

CHAPTER XI
WHERE IS BILLY RAY?

It seemed like the gang was walking for hours. They finally arrived at Billy Ray's house. Mary Jo looked across the road and motioned for B. J. to go up to the door. B. J. hurried through the gate and up on the porch. He lightly knocked at the door several times but did not get any answer. He put his ear to the door and listened for a sound but all he could hear was the sound of his heartbeat. Mary Jo, getting impatient, suggested that B. J. try to go around to the backyard. Quick as a flash, B. J. jumped from the porch and went around to the backyard. Mary Jo and the twins, looking exasperated, continued to hold their post at the gate.

In the meantime, B.J. came around from the backyard, telling Mary Jo no one was at home. The little gang began to wonder what happened to Billy Ray and his family. This was strange because someone was always at their house. Mary Jo had a strange expression on her face. Then all of a sudden she said, "oh, shucks, I forgot the women at the church are having a tea party and invited Billy Ray and his family."

Mary Jo could not do anything to stop the rage that was in B. J. at that moment. Even if she had his favorite treat. Everybody knows how much this boy loved strawberry kits, but the fierce feeling this boy was having, not even a kit would help. Mary Jo had the gang walk all the way out there in the hot sun. This was too much for B. J. to take, as he tried hard not to say anything to this girl for having him out in this hot, hot sun…changing colors. He did not need to add any color to his skin. He is fine just like he is. B. J. could not take it anymore as he yelled, "What, Mary Jo," as he began to stutter, "You, you, you got us all the way out he

The twins joined B. J., smartly saying, "Yeah! All the way out here." They were so upset with Mary Jo after all the praise they had just given her.

At this point, you could hear all of the frustration, disappointment, and the heat of the day. This was a bomber and the twins and B. J. let their leader know how they were feeling. They threw up their little hands feeling disgusted. Mary Jo has blown her leadership status with the little gang. B. J. was so upset that his glasses slid down to the tip of his nose. Looking over the top of the glasses, he asked, "Mary Jo, whose house did Billy Ray and his family go to?" He immediately pushed his glasses back upon his face and waited for a good answer. By this time, the little gang was even more mad. Mary Jo began hitting her forehead, trying to remember.

Actually, no one told her about the dinner. She was listening to grown folks conversation and overheard the women talking about it after church. Mary Jo knew she had to come up with something and in a hurry. The gang is not going to tolerate her nonsense anymore. She looked baffled as she tried to remember whose house Billy Ray's family was visiting. Mary Jo could feel the pressure from the gang. This was too much for Mary Jo and all she could do was let out a big sigh.

The twins, on the other hand, would not leave her alone, still suggesting Mary Jo was trying to put her hand under her chin. Maybe she could remember where Billy Ray is? Actually, the twins noticed Mary Jo on several occasions putting her hand under her chin. This seemed to help her remember what she had forgotten. Shirley and Sandy were definitely annoying, and Mary Jo was at her wits end when a light bulb flickered, causing her to remember. The women from the church were having a tea party and invited Billy's Ray family over too. Mary Jo was happy that she could remember.

After remembering where Billy Ray and his family were, Mary Jo dreaded the long walk over to Barbra's house. She lived way on the other side of town near the high school. The twins were not in favor of going way over there to whinny Barbra's house. Mary Jo gave the twins that look that the grown-ups use on their children. That did it. The twins started walking back up the path. B. J. stepped beside Mary Jo to let her know of a shorter way to get to Barbra's house.

This made the little spoiled twins happy. Mary Jo laughed as she noticed how the twins immediately stopped complaining and started questioning Mary Jo. "When are we going to get the money? Do we have some money saved in the Mason jar? What are we going to buy for Billy Ray?"

Mary Jo could not believe these twins asking her question without taking a breather. She had to raise her hand as if she was still in school to get the twin's attention. Finally getting the twins' attention, they stopped and stood there looking as if they were two little birds waiting to be fed. Taking a deep breath, Mary Jo explained to the twins that they would talk about it later. Most of all, she wanted the gift to be a surprise for Billy Ray. "Do not," as she hit the palm of her hand to get her point across, "talk about any of the questions you just asked." She went on to say that this will be Billy Ray's party not theirs, as they already had a bash of a party. This little gang is going to make Billy Ray's party the best party he ever had. The twins, looking up at Mary Jo, could not believe that she had all of those words in her. They knew she was smart but not like this. She had it all figured out so the twins agreed that they would not say anything.

They went down the path and followed it to the end, where the street began. The gang had not gone to the end of the path because they lived on that side of the street and there was no need to go farther. Most of their adventures were right in the area that they lived in. A new world was opening up to this little gang. Since they did not go to high school, they did not know this street was over here. They had to stay in the area that they lived in. This is a new world for them to explore.

You could hear the excitement in their voices, as they walked in the hot sun. The hot sun no longer mattered; they were in a new place. Looking at what they could have been doing made the walk shorter. They went down the walkway and saw a field with tall grass. There was a path right down the middle of it.

B. J. went down the path, as the girls followed behind, wondering where he was going. To their surprise, they could see a big house with a giant tree in the front yard. This was where Billy Ray and his family were.

Immediately, they started looking for Billy Ray. The twins saw Barbra sitting under the big tree. She jumped up waving and happy to see the girls. B. J. had enough of the girls and went looking for Billy Ray. Mary Jo headed up the stairs on the porch trying to find Billy Ray. Billy Ray was sitting at the end of the porch drinking some lemonade and looking bored. B. J. saw him first and ran across the porch to greet him. Billy Ray did not wait for him to get to him. He was out of that chair like a streak of lightning. Boy was he happy to see his friends.

CHAPTER XII
THE MASON JAR

Mary Jo did not enjoy getting up in the mornings. She liked to sleep until her mama woke her up for breakfast but most of the time, the smell from the food cooking in the kitchen would make her so hungry that she had to get up. On this particular morning, she was up before her mama even got out of bed. She had some thinking to do. Just lying around in bed was not helping her get the answers she needed. Her thoughts were on Billy Ray.

In six days, her friend would be leaving. The gang wanted to give him a going away party. How could they make some money for a party? What could they do? *It has to be something special,* Mary Jo thought. She eased her way off the side of the bed. Mary Jo quietly tiptoed across the cool wooden floor. The bathroom door squeaked, as she slowly closed it behind her. She felt the need to go outside and sit on the porch to think. With bare feet, she made her way outside to the front porch. She searched for a place where she would be able to feel the morning sun. The bottom of the steps was the perfect place. The sun felt good, as she sat down to wrap up in its warmth. She thought deeply, as she playfully drew circles in the damp dirt with her big toe. She was trying hard to think of a way to make some money.

What are we going to buy for Billy Ray after we get the money? Mary Jo thought. *It must be something special, nothing plain.* Her little mind continued to wonder, as she reminisced about the different things they did. She laughed aloud when she remembered the black hawk cherry incident. Mr. Sam came to her house and "spilled the beans." It was not funny then, but she could laugh about it now.

"Oh!" Mary Jo said, as the thought of Billy Ray leaving engulfed her heart. A little pain and sadness touched her heart. "Shucks!" Mary Jo said, feeling a little depressed, as she looked around to see if her mama was near. *Billy Ray will come back to see us,* she thought, but something deep inside of her knew he was never coming back.

The sun felt good, as it warmed her skinny body. She enjoyed the sun but in an instant, a shadow appeared. Looking up, she shaded her eyes to see if a cloud was covering the sun.

"Hey! Mary Jo!" B. J. said. "What are you doing sitting outside with no shoes on?"

Mary Jo sarcastically said, "Where did you come from B. J.? Get out of my sun."

"Look," he undauntedly said. Knowing that the sun belongs to everyone, B. J. made a point to ask, again, "where are your shoes?"

She impatiently said, "Would you just get out of my sun. B. J.? I am warming myself." Looking dumbfounded, he wondered why Mary Jo did not answer, even though he continued to block the sun. He did not understand why she was pestering him about the sun. Realizing B. J. was not going to move, she lazily moved to the other side of the steps. He slowly moved and decided to take a seat on the top step. Mary Jo was trying to think of a nice gift for Billy Ray. *Since B. J. is a boy, he could probably tell me what boys like to play with, or wear,*' she thought.

Clearing her throat, Mary Jo asked B.J. "What would be nice to get Billy Ray?"

Without waiting for an answer, she continued to ask him questions. "Arh, rah, ah, hum, Mary Jo. Give me time to think," he bluntly said.

Unmindful of what she was saying, Mary Jo blurted, "Oh shucks, B.J.!" Then, she quickly put her hand over her mouth. "I am not sitting out here just to get a suntan. I am thinking hard."

B.J. did not understand, as he dryly said, "I thought you were just enjoying the sun. Uh! You certainly do not need a tan." He laughed. "You got plenty of color. Plenty of color," as if repeating it made him feel good.

She arrogantly said, "B.J., I do not need you to tell me about my color."

He decided that it was best not to respond. He changed the subject and focused on what to get Billy Ray. "Well, even though you are a girl, Mary Jo, you seem to know a lot. What are we going to get Billy Ray, huh?" Then he came up with an idea.

B.J. told Mary Jo that Billy Ray was crazy about the army, cowboys and always wanted to ride on a train. Mary Jo jumped up, happy that she could choose from these three things. She now had something to work with. B.J. had a big smile on his face knowing he finally did something right. The excitement increased, as Mary Jo continued to play in the dirt. *Billy Ray needs something special,*' she thought.

B. J. sprung up and shouted. "Mary Jo, I know what we can get him!"

"What?" she asked, not too interested in what his answer would be.

"Well," as he stood like a cowboy, talking out of the corner of his mouth. "We can get him a watch," he calmly said.

Mary Jo slapped her leg and said "Gosh lee! That's it, B. J." Rubbing her head, she thought, why didn't she think of that since she has all the brains.

B. J. was about to steal his glory back. He said, "Mary Jo, how come you did not think of this?" He was grinning, from ear to ear, as he sat back down on the step. *At last,* he thought, *I got Miss Smarty.* The sun reflected off his glasses and indeed, this was the moment for B. J. to glow. It did not seem to faze Mary Jo, as she sat with her arms folded.

Looking up, she sharply said, "B.J., what kind of watch should we get him?"

"Uh! Ah, uh, I know," B. J. said. "How about a Hop-along Cassidy? No, no wait, Gene Autry, or Dick Tracy."

Mary Jo, jumping up and down, said, "Please! B. J. make up your mind." She quickly sat back down and continued to play in the dirt with her big toe.

Under his breath B. J. mumbled, "I cannot believe it. She said, 'please.'"

Mary Jo, not quite understanding him, asked, "What did you say, B. J?"

"Uh, nothing," B. J. said.

Feeling perturbed, she went into her smart aleck mood. "You know, Mr. Smarty-Pants. I think we need to get together first. Then we can decide what watch to buy. Is that alright with you, B.J.?"

Why did she go and call B. J. "Mr. Smarty-Pants" again? She was about to start another war between them. Mary Jo knew calling him, that name was a no, no. Immediately, with anger in his voice, said, "Don't you dare call me that anymore, do you hear me?"

Mary Jo was frightened to say anything, as she looked at B. J. ranting and raving about a nickname. Trying to smooth things over, Mary Jo softly said, "Well B. J., after all, you're the smartest boy in class. Remember, huh, huh?"

"Un! I never thought of it like that, Mary Jo." B.J. thought about it and decided to leave it alone. He regained his composure and wanted to know how much dough was in the treasure.

Mary Jo could not tell B. J. because she had to go get the money. She quietly went upstairs to the attic. She looked in her secret hiding place and picked up the Mason jar, looking around to see if anyone heard her come upstairs. *Good*, she thought. *No one saw me.* Mary Jo carefully held up the jar and peeked inside. There was a shiny quarter at the bottom of the jar.

Feeling dismayed, she could not believe this was all the gang had. She thought this *would only buy each of us a bottle of soda pop.* She began to wonder where the money would come from.

She hurried back outside where B. J. was waiting eagerly. He was smiling when Mary Jo approached him, but she looked disappointed. B. J. was so thrilled that he did not notice the sour look on her face. Before he could ask her, she gave him the bad news. They did not have very much money. "Uh, uh, how much money did you say we have, huh, huh?" He asked.

Mary Jo, staring at the not so full jar, replied, "Not much."

B. J. anxiously said, "How much is not much Mary Jo?"

Mary Jo looked up at the sky, as if to find the answer. "Let me see," she said with her hand under her chin. With a burst of energy, she said, "How about a quarter?" She held the jar up so he could see the shiny quarter in the bottom.

"Wow!" B. J. said. "Mary Jo, a watch costs $4.95 so that means we need to get $4.70 more, huh?"

In deep thought, Mary Jo coldly said, "Yeah! B. J., I can count," as she continued to play in the dirt.

CHAPTER XIII
AFTER WE GET THE MONEY

Wondering what Mary Jo was going to do, B.J. anxiously asked himself, *where in the world are we going to get that kind of money?* A thought crossed his mind and he laughed, as he knew what grown-ups would tell him. He could hear them saying, "Boy, you better get out there and pull some weeds; pick up somebody's yard, wash somebody's dog, etc."

He laughed, as he thought of how to make some money. At this point, Mary Jo could not think of anything. B.J. was sitting and thinking that the smartest girl in the class could not think of a way to make some money. He put his hands behind his head and watched her still make circles in the dirt.

"You know what, B. J.?" Mary Jo said excitedly, "I bet that my mama could tell us how to make some money. Cause you know grown-ups like to work."

After hearing Mary Jo's suggestion, B. J.'s brain began to work. They could ask Mary Jo's mother how they could make some money to buy Billy Ray a nice gift. B. J. said, "Don't forget to tell your mother we need the money quickly." B. J. 's eyes lit up like fireworks, knowing their idea would work.

Mary Jo was relieved that they had finally found a solution to their problem. She paused, let out a sigh and vainly said, "At last, my brain is working. Coming outside in the fresh morning air has cleared my brain. I am getting all kinds of good ideas, B.J."

He had a blank look on his face. "What did the outside have to do with her coming up with an idea? After all, I helped her get the idea," he mumbled to himself.

"Oh! B. J." Mary Jo exclaimed. "Let's go get the twins' Red Flyer wagon. We can go look for some pop bottles to sell. Maybe we can get some scrap metal or rags too."

"Yeah!" B. J. shouted. "I knew you would come up with something to do." B. J. was so happy that he ran off without Mary Jo. She stood up, shaking her head and wondered *where in the world did his mama get him.* She shook her head thinking, *that boy is so smart that he's dumb-d-u-m-b! Why didn't he wait for me to get my shoes?* She quickly ran upstairs to get her shoes. Her mama was up, getting ready to cook her breakfast. After getting her shoes, Mary Jo went into the kitchen to tell her mama the news. "Billy Ray and his whole family are moving," she anxiously said.

Mrs. Hattie stopped what she was doing and said, "Child, where yoes git dat notion from, huh?"

"Mama, when we were coming home last night, Billy Ray told us. The family is moving to Detroit, Michigan. His daddy got a job making cars."

Surprised by what Mary Jo had just said, Mrs. Hattie was speechless. She picked up the big iron skillet and put it on the stove. Shaking her head, she said, "Uh, ah," as if trying to ask Mary Jo something else, but she could not find the words.

Mary Jo told her what Billy Ray had told them. "His uncle, Claude's wife died not too long ago. He wanted his daddy to come up there and live with him for a while. Billy Ray's uncle worked at the car factory. He helped get Billy Ray's dad a job there, too."

"Lard, Lard," Mrs. Hattie said. "Dat shore is good for Ethel and dem kids. Theys will have a good house to live in now. Maybe wes women can fix a nice dinner for dem. Uh! hum. When will deys bes leavin, child?"

"In six days, Mama," Mary Jo replied. "And Mama, can you help the gang get some money to buy Billy Ray a watch?"

"Shore child, wes can have a fish fry. Uh-hum! Shore can. How much money yoes got Mary Jo?"

Mary Jo sheepishly said, "A quarter Mama."

Mrs. Hattie let out a big laugh and said, "Mary Jo, a quarter? Dat wont hardy git a pop."

Mary Jo proudly said, "We are going to get some pop bottles and sell them. Maybe we can look for some scrap metal or rags."

Her Mama thought about what Mary Jo had just said and figured it was a good idea. Her Mama hugged Mary Jo and let her know that she was proud of what they wanted to do for their friend. In the meantime, Mary Jo happily thanked her mama and let her know that she got that from her. Mrs. Hattie is good at helping people around town whenever there is a need. Mary Jo quickly took a seat at the table and let her mama finish fixing her breakfast.

In front of Mary Jo, was a biscuit, blackberry jelly and country butter; the sweet kind you get from the country store. There was also a cold glass of milk and freshly made juice. She smelled the country ham, sausage patties and fried sunny side up eggs that were soon to grace the table. Whenever Mary Jo would go over to someone else's house she'd politely decline when offered food. Mrs. Hattie made sure that Mary Jo would not embarrass her by accepting food from others. If you were invited, then it was alright, and they taught their children this rule.

Mary Jo had wasted enough time, so she grabbed a biscuit sandwich. Mrs. Hattie was surprised as she saw Mary Jo heading for the door with two biscuit sandwiches in her hand. She let her mama know that she needed to meet the gang at the twin's house, and she would be back later. All Mrs. Hattie could hear from Mary Jo was a mumbling sound as she continued out the front door. She stopped long enough to take a bite of her biscuit sandwich and lick the butter that ran down her wrist.

The sun was getting hotter, as she skipped down the road. "This is going to be a good day to get Billy Ray a watch," she said. She pondered which watch to get him. "Let me see," Mary Jo said, as she continued talking to herself. "A Dick Tracy watch is nice but that is not Billy Ray."

In the meantime, the butter on the biscuit was running down her arm again. What a mess she made with that biscuit. Mary Jo licked the butter and jelly off her hand and arm, she looked at her hands to see if she had gotten all of the jelly and butter off. She spotted B. J. pulling the little red wagon up the road. Mary Jo stopped and put her hands on those two bony hips. She waited for him to come to her. As he got closer, B. J. had a look of disgust on his face.

Mary Jo, getting into her act again, asked B. J. why he did not wait until she could get her shoes on. "Huh, huh, Mr. Smarty pants?"

By this time, B. J. was so angry with Mary Jo that she could smell his hot breath with a stale odor of strawberry kit going up her nose. "You need to stop calling me smarty-pants and this is the last time I am going to tell you." He was beating his fist in his other hand to let Mary Jo know 'enough was enough.' "The boys are tired of you silly girls and that is it."

Beads of sweat were popping out on his face and forehead, as he stood there eyeing Mary Jo. She was not really paying too much attention to what B. J. was saying however, to keep the peace, she said, "O.k."

B. J. did not want to get into a big discussion with her. He informed her that he left her because it did not take long to get the wagon. Mary Jo followed him, as he pulled the little red wagon down the path.

Mary Jo thought to herself, *this little gang really needs me,* as she stopped motionless in her glory thinking she helped B. J. see the light. Does the gang really need a second mama?

CHAPTER XIV
POP BOTTLES AND SCRAP METAL

The sun got hotter, as Mary Jo and B.J. pulled the little red wagon. They needed to start looking for some pop bottles and scrap metal, if they wanted to get some money for Billy Ray's gift. Both decided that they would look where the rich white folks lived first. Usually, they found some good stuff in that part of town. Along the way, they found a coke bottle and an old cooking pan with a big hole in it. B. J. stopped, excitedly, he got an idea. They could make a lot of money just by finding scrap metal.

Mary Jo must have read his mind, as sharply asked him, "Where are we going to find scrap metal, B. J.?"

"Uh! Ah, uh," he said. This boy was acting as if something had gotten his tongue. Mary Jo waited for B. J. to get it together. Finally, he pointed to the trash can and excitedly said, "Mary Jo, you know it's a drive on scrap metal because of the war. We could get rich just selling it."

Jumping up and down, the thought hit B. J. and he knew they had a chance to be rich. Mary Jo could not believe what she was seeing. A thought quickly crossed her smart mind. She thought, *what in this world is wrong with B. J.? There he is jumping up and down in the hot sun.*

Out of breath from all of the unnecessary jumping, he finally said, "We could be rich!" Mary Jo did not think his idea was that great. She stopped and looked at him. The excitement rose in his voice as he explained it to her. "We should look for scrap metal everywhere and think of all the money we could get. Hot dog!" B. J. shouted, not really paying attention to what he just said.

Nevertheless, Mary Jo was determined to have her say about B. J. using words he should not say. With her hands on her bony hips, she informed B. J. that "hot dog" was as if you were cursing. B. J. threw a question right back at her. "Since you know so much about the Bible, what book is that in, huh? Let me hear it." Mary Jo was dumbfounded at this boy asking her a question like that. A little laugh rose up out of her. This boy is getting smarter and smarter. "Oh, for

Pete's sake! Mary Jo, don't you eat hotdogs?" Standing, as if in a daze, Mary Jo could not remember whether that was in the Bible or if it was something the grown-ups came up with. She could not think of a good answer, so she decided to leave it alone. B. J. could not believe he finally made his point.

Mary Jo went on to tell B. J. it would be alright to look for scrap metal although it is easier to look for pop bottles. "You know B. J.; people are always walking in these alleys drinking pop on their way home from work. They just throw them away most of the time."

Not really listening to what Mary Jo had to say, B. J. continued thinking about his idea for scrap metal. Mary Jo welled up inside but said nothing. B. J. was on it now. He threw up his hands, as the idea hit him again.

Mary Jo did not see the need for B. J.to be so happy. They needed to get busy hunting for some pop bottles. Mary Jo was wondering why B. J. was putting his hands up. Did the Spirit hit him out here in this hot sun? *Hum! That only happens at church,* she thought to herself. "Why did you have your hands up, B. J., huh? Did something happen to you?"

B.J. could not believe this girl and that entire silly question she asked him. The sun has definitely fried her brain today. "Oh, nothing. I was just thinking how much money we could make, that is all," B.J. said.

He quickly started searching in the tall grass and under the bushes for those pop bottles people throw away. While looking under the brushes, he spotted an old metal pipe. "See, see, Mary Jo," he said. "We got to hunt for scrap metal. It is all over the place."

For the most part, she only noticed one piece but was convinced that maybe they should spend their time looking for scrap metal. They found two pieces of broken metal lying right in the alleyway. B.J. was overjoyed as they continued to look in trash cans and in the tall grass. They even found an old pair of glasses that used to belong to someone. B.J. and Mary Jo searched everywhere until the little red wagon was filled with junk. They decided they had enough and headed up town to the scrap metal yard.

The sun seemed to have gotten hotter, as they looked down the street and saw the big sign that read *Iron & Scrap Metal Yard*. B. J. was excited about how much money they were going to make. They pulled their little red wagon up to the scales so the man could weigh the metal. He looked down at Mary Jo and B. J. and asked, "What do we have here? How much metal do you have?" Mary Jo solidly looked at the old man and wondered why he was asking all those questions.

Immediately, B. J spoke up and said, "about one dollar worth, huh, Mary Jo?" During this time, Mary Jo was quiet, as she did not feel like answering B. J. and the old man's silly questions. She just gave them that look.

The old man weighed their metal on the scales. It will let Mary Jo and B. J. know how much money they would get. "Hum!" the old man said. "At three cents a pound and eight pounds, which will be twenty-four cents."

B. J. shouted, "twenty-four cents, Mary Jo? All that work for twenty-four cents?"

Mary Jo wanted to laugh because B.J.'s easy money idea did not work as well as he thought. However, to make him feel better, she said, "Hey, B.J., we have six pop bottles. These bottles are worth five cents apiece, not like your rich scrap metal, B.J."

"Yeah!" B. J. calmly said. He was feeling a little disgusted that he did not get the money they needed. B. J. did not say anything but thought to himself, *all that work for just 49 cents. That is a long way from four dollars and ninety-five cents.*

This boy was not getting it, as frustration kicked in. Mary Jo and all that adding she was doing, with no money did not make sense. B. J. said angrily, "What is the dollars for?" "Huh, huh?"

"Boy!" Mary Jo said, "You do not know anything about shopping." Mary Jo's mother would take her to the store with her and point out things she would need and pay for the items. She continued to explain how much is spent like twenty-five cents worth of winter trout, ten cents worth lard, fifteen cents, for a loaf of Miss Sunbeam Bread. "Now, we can go on to the store and get the fish and other things. We'll come back later if we need to." B. J. understood what Mary Jo was going to do. He smiled, as another idea crossed his mind.

CHAPTER XV
MR. BOB'S STORE

After hearing Mary Jo explain how to spend the money they made from the junkyard, B.J. was happy. He even acknowledged that Mary Jo knew how to shop. In that moment of glory, she walked down the road with grandeur to Mr. Bob's store. She was in her own little world of happiness. Suddenly, she stopped and said, "Gosh lee! This is going to be a great day to have a fish fry."

"Who told you, huh Mary Jo?" B. J. asked, looking puzzled. "Yeah, yeah" he said as if he was trying to convince himself. "I guess this is a good day, Mary Jo."

B. J. continued thinking about how much money they could make, however, Mary Jo decided to do some figuring of her own. They walked along the road, as Mary Jo thought about how many pieces of fish, they could get for seventy-five cents. If Mr. Bob was nice today, maybe he would give them ten whole fish. "And, and" as the excitement rose in her voice, she yelled, "My mama can cut the fish in half and get twenty pieces."

She was beside herself now and on a roll. That would give them enough money to buy Billy Ray a very nice gift. Mary Jo felt good about B. J. and getting the money for a gift. B.J. stopped and did some thinking himself. Mary Jo had a good idea. Twenty fish sandwiches would give them ten dollars or more. This really made B. J. shout out "Hot dog! We have done gone and made us some money!"

Here this boy is standing out in the hot sun acting like a kid again. Immediately, Mary Jo corrected B. J.'s bad English and said, "just hold on, we have not sold any fish sandwiches yet."

Nevertheless, Mary Jo was thinking, and she let Mr. Smarty Pants know it. You could hear the sharpness in her voice. She did a no-no when her angry words called B. J. the forbidden name. You could hear the grinding of his teeth. Beating his fist in his hand, his horn-rimmed glasses slid down his nose. This really upset B. J. He was madder than two hens fighting in the rain. This time Mary Jo had gone too far. This boy has had enough of her smart cracks.

"Do not call me that, Mary Jo." He stood there with beads of sweat popping off of his forehead. He was standing in the middle of the road ready to square off with this girl. She is just too smart for her own pants. He was trying to figure out why this girl always called him 'Mr. Smarty Pants.'

"No one else in the gang even mentions that I am smart but her. Ugh!" He kicked the dirt again. "I cannot help it if I like science and insects," he said to himself.

This was Mary Jo's que to take off walking as fast as she could. She thought B. J. is hotter than red pepper now. Mary Jo did not want to be around him in that state of mind. B. J. had to run to catch up with her. He waited until he was right beside her and let her have it. B. J. was mad as he called her by her whole name, "Mary Jo Ruth Finney." This was unlike him to use her whole name. The atmosphere around them was filled with anger. It was as if a war was about to start. A field of gloom entered their space. You could hear the anger in his voice. He shouted out, "No more Mary Jo! Stop calling me Smarty Pants, you hear me?"

Mary Jo must have forgotten those summer days in mid-July are the hottest. She's standing there with this boy who is madder than a wet hen. He is shouting in her face with his hot breath and spit flying out his mouth. Mary Jo got his message loud and clear and politely said she was sorry and assured him it wouldn't happen again.

There was a quiet stillness in the atmosphere after B. J. stopped yelling at Mary Jo. She was thinking this boy is really mad. He never called her by her whole name. Mary Jo could not say anything, as she watched B.J. wipe the sweat off of his face with his T-shirt. This boy had the audacity to get in the star's face and shout what she had better not do anymore. You can bet Mary Jo saw a side of B.J. she had never seen. She learned that boys really do get mad at girls.

All was finally well, and Mary Jo needed to tell B. J. that they should share the money with her mama. "It is not fair to take all the money when she will be doing all the work. We should not keep it all for ourselves."

Slowly giving her an answer, B. J. said, "Uh, you are right Mary Jo. Your mama should get some money too."

Huh! What would these boys do without me? Mary Jo thought. Still thinking, she knows everything as she smiled. B. J. noticed the look she had on her face but decided not to respond.

As Mary Jo approached Mr. Bob's store, she noticed something shiny in the doorway. She quickly reached down and picked it up. Mary Jo showed it to B. J. It was a half dollar. She opened her hand so he could see it. She was elated as she went into the store. She acted as if she had a hundred dollars in her pocket, instead of a dollar and forty-nine cents.

B.J. was acting as if he were cheering for his favorite team. He was yelling "yeah, yeah" to himself. Counting the money Mary Jo had, B. J. figured they could get everything now. He assumed they'd even have some change left. Smiling. "Uh! Uh! Uh!" He said, acting as if he was a little kid. Mary Jo knew B. J. was waiting for her to ask him if he wanted some money for some kits. This boy loved strawberry kits and would do anything to get some. When at the store, he would always buy four packs of kits. All he wanted was four cents of the money.

Since Mary Jo had been rough on him, she decided to buy him four packs of his favorite strawberry kits. She gave B. J. four pennies, and he went straight to the candy counter and looked for them. She went to the other counter where Mr. Bob was standing and gave him her order. Mr. Bob, grunting as usual, looked up from the paper and read the order, "Small loaf of bread…" but before he could continue, Mary Jo interrupted him.

"Oh! No Mr. Bob, you, better give me a large loaf of bread."

Mr. Bob pointed to the rack behind her and told her to get a large loaf. B. J. did not want to miss out on getting his kits, so he hurried over to the rack and got a large loaf of bread. He placed the bread on the counter and continued looking at his kits.

B.J. wanted his kits. Mary Jo sensed that B.J. did not want to wait while Mr. Bob read her list. She asked Mr. Bob if he could give B.J. four packs of kits next. A big smile crossed his face as he waited. Mr. Bob looked over his glasses which were sitting on the end of his nose. "Fine, fine, Mary Ruth," he said.

She hated being called Mary Ruth, but Mr. Bob seemed to enjoy calling her that. She thought, *there he goes with that Mary Ruth mess again.* She dared not say anything to grown folks about what they say. That definitely was a no, no. Mr. Bob continued to read Mary Jo's little note as if she had a whole list of items. Mary Jo looked up at him as he read "seventy-five cents worth of winter trout."

Mary Jo was quick to interrupt him again, "No, Mr. Bob, you had better make that a dollar's worth." She noticed B. J. standing there with his nose pressed against the glass. Mr. Bob stopped waiting on Mary Jo and went to the counter where B. J. was standing and reached into the case and took out four packages of strawberry kits. This boy was as happy as he thanked Mr. Bob. He immediately opened a pack and put two in his mouth. Mr. Bob went back to the meat counter with Mary Jo slowly following him. At the counter, Mary Jo pressed her face to the cool glass. Mr. Bob picked out the winter trout covered with chipped ice.

"Here now, Mary Ruth!" Mr. Bob said, as he reached over the big freezer to hand her the fish and remind her to tell her mama that the fish was fresh, right off the boat. "The fish came in this morning. You hear me, Mary Ruth."

She carefully took the package, thanking him again. Mary Jo quickly left the store, as B. J. followed behind her. She was in a hurry, and it was hard for B. J. to keep up. He was too busy eating kits. "Hum-um- hum!" he delightfully said.

This girl was so far ahead of B. J. that she had to stop and wave for him to come on. B. J. grumbled, looking up at the road between the heat waves, shouting for Mary Jo to slow down. He was really smacking, as he got closer to Mary Jo. All she could hear were sounds of "Mm-mm-mm! Hum!" coming from B. J.'s mouth.

"B.J.", Mary Jo said firmly as she popped her lips. "Do you have to smack so loud?"

Between his munching, B. J. said, "I cannot help it if I like strawberry kits, Mary Jo. I am trying to get all of the strawberry flavor out of them. Anyway, what is the big rush? Why are we walking so fast, huh, Mary Jo?"

CHAPTER XVI
A GIRL AND A CAT NAMED TOM

Hot and bothered, Mary Jo pointed to the package and said, "B. J., you know the railroad men will be coming at four o'clock today and mama needs to clean the fish." He decided to kick at the rocks and dirt again.

This was fun as he tried to see how far he could kick rocks and dirt. This did not sit too well with Mary Jo, as she hurried along beside him. She could taste the dust that B. J. kept stirring up. She decided not to pay any attention to this kid and thought, "What's the use? He is just having fun."

During this time, B.J. was not paying too much attention to her. His little mind started to think about how much money they could possibly make. He was excited and wanted to ask Mary Jo about the money. He got his nerve up and cleared his throat and said, "By the way, Mary Jo, we are going to make a lot of money today, huh?"

She thought, *this kid has really been in the sun too long. It must be all that sugar from them kits getting to him. Yeah, I bet that's it.* She hastily walked toward the path to her house.

B.J. did not want to eat his last pack of kits because he wanted to save them for later. The weather was too hot, and he did not want them to melt, so he took out two kits and put them in his mouth. Mary Jo was not in any mood to look at B.J., as he ate his kits. He had to run to catch up with her. He shouted, "Mary Jo, do you know what watch we can get Billy Ray, huh?"

"No!" Mary Jo sharply said. "I have not really thought about it. We have to get some money first, O. K.?"

Like a little kid, B.J. did not say anything else but agreed she was right. Little did Mary Jo know; a surprise was waiting for her on the path.

Tom was a chubby cat with a golden, yellowish, black-striped body, eyes like a tiger, a black nose and a mysterious-looking something on his forehead. He would pay her a surprise visit today. While Tom the cat enjoys sleeping on the path, the grass has always been a question

for those who walk this path. Mostly older people take this route up the path coming home from work.

Generally, you can find Tom getting his much-needed rest in the middle of the pathway, or lying on his back, catching some sun rays but, on this particular day the wind was slightly blowing, and the smell of fresh fish had crossed old Tom's nose. Oh, this cat must be dreaming. Did he really smell some fish?

"Ah! Ah," old Tom must be wondering as he continued to sleep. Then it happened again. A nippy, swift breeze blew his way again. Old Tom sprang to his feet like a sprinter getting ready for a race. His front paws automatically spread out. He leaned like a racer getting ready to come out of the starting block. Then, with his head held high and his nose pointed forward sniffing the odorous air, Tom sensed that the scent of fish was getting closer and closer. He excitedly anticipated the taste of his meal. Tom's tail was like a pendant swinging back and forth, as if ready to strike the time of day.

Just a cat's paw away from where Mary Jo was walking, she carefully carried her package. She had it tucked neatly under her right arm, holding the bag with her hand. Minding her business, she rushed to get home with the fish. Her friend B.J. was just straggling behind her again. He was in his own little world, savoring his last pack of strawberry kits.

Walking hastily, Mary Jo thought about which watch they should buy Billy Ray. She was in such deep thought that she did not notice anything of the ordinary. Old Tom's nose caught the scent of the fresh fish again, and like a flash of lighting, he jumped on Mary Jo. Startled and knocked down to the ground, Mary Jo did not know what was going on. She was unable to figure out what had just happened and why B.J. could not come to Mary Jo's aid. B.J. could see the commotion but was overcome with laughter. All he could do was laugh, as the tears were running down his face. He held his stomach, as Mary Jo called his name.

"B. J., B. J., B. J. Get this dumb cat off me!" She yelled helplessly, as her voice grew faint. The poor thing was left to fight off an evil cat that was trying to take her fish. Mary Jo's friend was not in any shape to help her. He was lying on the ground laughing like a hyena. He thought it was like seeing World War III in the path. There was a war going on between Mary Jo and a cat named Tom. What a sight to see; Mary Jo fiercely fighting and yelling at B.J, and at the same time, unsympathetically kicking and yelling at Tom.

This did not deter that old cat from trying to get the package Mary Jo had under her arm. Tom was acting like his ancestors, fiercely tearing at the package. He was struggling trying to open it with his paws. Tom was making snarling sounds to scare Mary Jo. However, she was not giving up that easily.

In the midst of the battle, Mary Jo somehow got ahold of Tom's tail and furiously tossed him over into the tall grass. Tom was stunned and surprised by Mary Jo's quick move. You could not see him at this point, but you could hear him in the tall grass, feebly crying, "meow, meow," like a wounded victim that had narrowly escaped a battle.

Mary Jo is overcome by events and traumatized by Tom's actions. She picked up her package and hurriedly took off running and yelling for her mama. She yelled so loud; you could hear her on the next block. "Mama, Mama, oh Mama, come quick old Tom is trying to kill me." He was not trying to kill her. All Tom wanted was the package of fish, but you could not convince Mary Jo of that.

Upon hearing the urgency in her voice, Mrs. Hattie ran nervously to the back door. She wanted to know what the fuss was about. Mrs. Hattie began calling out, "Mary Jo!" as she ran down the steps. "Child, whats de matters with my baby?"

"Mama, mama, mama," half out of breath, Mary Jo said. "Tom was trying to take my fish. He is over there in that grass somewhere." Mrs. Hattie looked around trying to figure out what in the world her child was talking about. She affectionately placed her warm cushion arms around Mary Jo and softly comforted her. She held Mary Jo for a moment, letting her know that everything was all right.

Mrs. Hattie asked Mary Jo, "What happened child?"

Mary Jo, looking bewildered, said in an unflustered voice, "Mama, Tom jumped on me and tried to take the package of fish. I tossed him over there in the grass." Mrs. Hattie lovingly helped Mary Jo walk wobbly into the house and sat her in a chair at the kitchen table.

Mrs. Hattie, in her motherly way said, "Mary Jo baby, cats just like fish, OK?" Mary Jo, looking up at her mama sadly nodded her head. "Tom was just trying to get something he liked, dats all, baby," her mama said.

Her mama took the fish and laid it on the table to clean them. Mary Jo, after having regained her composure, decided to watch her mama clean the fish. Her eyes were on her mama, but she still could not believe him. She could still picture B.J. not lifting a hand to help her. He just laid down on the ground laughing hysterically. Pondering these thoughts made Mary Jo even more mad. As she sat tense and perturbed, her chubby little fist balled up. In the meantime, B.J. was standing at the back door wondering whether to go in or stay outside. Mary Jo knew he was at the door but continued to watch her mama prepare the fish.

Finally, he got up enough nerve to knock on the screen door. Mrs. Hattie turned from the table and told Mary Jo to let Sonny boy in. Mary Jo, scuffing her feet, slowly walked across the wooden kitchen floor. She opened the screen door and stared at B. J. B. J. softly said, "I am sorry, Mary Jo."

Mary Jo responded with a sharp tongue and a stern look on her face, "B.J.! That is not good enough." She was out for blood, as she irately mimicked her teacher by putting her finger on his nose. She then said, "B. J., you ought to be ashamed of yourself. You were laughing as if you had gone mad while Tom was trying to kill me."

Being undaunted, and standing up to Mary Jo, B. J. said, "How do you know? For Pete's sake Mary Jo, Tom was not trying to do no such a thing."

Mary Jo said, "You do not know how cats act? B. J." Knowing that any verbal response would make her even angrier, he refused to open his mouth and proceeded to remove her finger off his nose. He quickly walked over to the kitchen table, out of reach of her irritating tongue.

CHAPTER XVII
TOO CLOSE FOR COMFORT

Mary Jo continued to follow B. J., keeping her body directly in his face. She was so close that she could smell the scent of the strawberry kits still on his breath. Her eyes were throwing daggers and her mouth was blowing out hot air. B. J. did not give into her taunting, mentally manipulating body language. He knew she was too close, and he did not know what was on her mind. Even though her mama was in the kitchen with him, he did not feel comfortable around her. Nevertheless, he decisively stood his ground, while looking at Mary Jo's scowling face.

Suddenly, Mrs. Hattie turned, looked at Mary Jo and asked, "Mary Jo, has yoes lost yore mind girl?"

Mrs. Hattie said again, "If yoes do not gat out of sonny boy's face, yoes better." Mary Jo, feeling embarrassed, walked over to the kitchen table and flopped down in a chair giving B.J. that look again and rudely stuck her tongue out at him.

Mary Jo was really aggravated. She feared punishment from her mama, so she momentarily closed her mouth and rolled her eyes at B. J. He was not concerned, as he smiled at Mary Jo. He was glad that Mrs. Hattie was near to help him out of this mess but Mary Jo was not through with him yet. She taunted the poor boy with those eyes of hers. With her lips poked out, she went to get her favorite drink. She went over to get some Kool-Aid out of the icebox. She smugly walked back to the table with an attitude and slumped down in her chair.

Meanwhile, B. J. continued to smirk at her. The atmosphere in the kitchen made Mrs. Hattie uneasy. She turned from the sink and noticed that Mary Jo was not being polite. She did not ask B. J. if he would like a glass of Kool-Aid. Mary Jo was still upset with B.J. and she definitely was not thinking about giving him a glass of Kool-Aid.

Immediately Mrs. Hattie said "Mary Jo! Where is yore manners young girl? Give sonny boy some Kool-Aid too."

"But Mama," Mary Jo quickly said, "B. J. does not want any Kool-Aid. Do you B. J.?"

B.J. almost jumped out of his seat because Mar Jo had finally been caught being rude. He gladly said, "Sure Mary Jo, I would like a glass of cold Kool-Aid." This intensified Mary Jo's anger, as she gave him the look.

Repeating herself, Mrs. Hattie told Mary Jo to get Sonny boy a glass of Kool-Aid. Mary Jo was steaming, as she got up from the table. Mary Jo wanted to ring B.J.'s neck like a chicken. In the meantime, Mrs. Hattie went to the back porch to get something. She was tired and wanted the mess to be finished. As soon as her mama went out the back door, Mary Jo mischievously ran back to the table. She almost tripped over a chair as she whispered, "B.J., why did you not help me?"

B.J. gathered his thoughts as he sipped on his Kool-Aid and noticed that she was still mad at him. Then he said sincerely in a sheepish voice, "Mary Jo, I am sorry."

Mary Jo rolled her big brown eyes and felt fiendishly proud of herself because B. J. had apologized. Not letting this thing go she said, "Tom could have killed me, B. J. and my mama would be mad at you." B. J. carefully and conscientiously leaned across the table and said, "Nobody ever gotten killed by Tom."

Wanting proof that a cat can kill you, Mary Jo asked her mama as she returned to the kitchen. "Mama, Mama," Mary Jo said, as her mama came back into the room. "Is that true what B.J. said, Mama?"

Her mama gave her a low "Uh, hum! Mary Jo." Her mama was not too concerned with her and B. J.'s conversation. She was busy trying to get the fish cleaned and seasoned.

Mary Jo did not care that her mama was busy with getting the fish ready. "B. J. said that" as she got louder, making sure her mama could hear her. "Is it true that cats can take your breath too? Huh Mama?"

"Uh hum!" Mrs. Hattie said. Mary Jo refused to accept her mama's answer. She was acting like a man trying to make a 'dead horse get up and run' even though he is dead.

Mrs. Hattie left, and Mary Jo took the opportunity to get up from the table. She was not really paying attention to the never-ending arguing from the children. She had her mind on getting the fish ready before the railroad men came. The fish needed to be covered so Mrs. Hattie took a dish towel to put over the pan of fish. Those annoying flies would have a good time getting a free meal. She went out the back door to give Tom the cat a much-needed dinner. After the big fight he had with Mary Jo, he most likely was trying to get his breath. Poor thing what a day this has been for him. All he was trying to do was get a nap and get some sun rays. What a life? To be treated as if he was a dog.

Mary Jo took the opportunity to get up from the table. She gave B. J. a piece of her mind. Putting her hands on those two bony hips and rocking from side to side she let him have it. "Hattie ain't around to protect you now, Sonny boy", she said, pointing her finger in his face.

B. J. was so outdone at the disrespect she was showing her mother by calling her "Hattie."

He jumped from his chair and said, "Mary Jo! I am going to tell your mama you called her Hattie."

Infuriated by this remark, Mary Jo came around the table so fast that B. J.'s eyes got as big as his lens in his glasses. She was furious and said with her face in his face, "Go ahead and tell B. J. I will get you" as she placed that finger on his nose again. She backed off from him and said again, "I will get you."

B.J. could not believe his eyes. He looked at her as if she was Dr. Jeckle and Mr. Hide. This was a monster movie they went to see one Saturday. She went from Mary Jo to wanting to get B. J. She turned and told B. J. again "Go head and see Sonny boy"

This was worse than her and that cat. What happened to the two of them was over, but she wouldn't leave it alone.

CHAPTER XVIII
MARY JO MISBEHAVING

Mary Jo had a little World War III going on with B. J., even though let her know he was sorry. Mary Jo wanted revenge and until she received justice, there would be no peace. She starred offensively, at B. J. as she walked out the door. She went to see what her mama was doing.

Although, puzzled by Mary Jo's irrational behavior, B. J. got up from the table and stood at the screen door. Looking at Mary Jo talking to her mother about Tom, B. J. took off his glasses to clean the lenses. Mary Jo had poked her bony finger at him so much that day, he could not see clearly out of them.

He pressed his face against the screen and silently laughed. *I was going to marry her when I grew up, but not now. That girl will fight a dog if he gets in her way."* B.J. laughed at the thought.

Then he heard Mrs. Hattie say, "Mary Jo!" as she walked toward the front yard. Tom the cat was walking right on her heels. "Tell Sonny boy to get de iron pot and bring it to the front yard."

"You keep your distance." He played it safe by staying away from Mary Jo. "Yes ma'am, Mama." Mary Jo said, "I'll tell him."

B.J. heard everything Mrs. Hattie said but was not in any hurry to get another tongue lashing from Mary Jo. He decided to play it safe behind the screen door. Mary Jo was walking toward the shed yelling out, "B.J., B.J.! You can come out now. Mama wants you to bring the iron pot around to the front yard."

B.J., moving as slow as a snail, slid open the screen door and walked down the steps. At the same time, he was consciously taking notice of Mary Jo going into the woodshed. Running like a track runner, he picked up the heavy pot. He was hurrying toward the house and hoping Mary Jo would not come out of the woodshed. Mary Jo found the charcoal, emerged from the woodshed and noticed B. J. struggling with the iron pot. "B. J.!" Mary Jo called out startling him. "Would you like some help?"

The sound of her voice made him almost drop the iron pot. He sat it down and said, "No, Mary Jo, this is a man's job."

Mary Jo snappily walked over to where B. J. was standing and said, "Why must you always think you are a man, huh B. J.?"

"Mary Jo, this is why I am a man," as he flexed his two bony arms. He almost fainted trying to push his scrawny chest out. B. J. was trying to hold an already flat stomach in. Still full of drama, Mary Jo threw her hands up in the air. She looked angrily at him and walked around to the other side of the house with the charcoal.

In the meantime, Mrs. Hattie was busy putting her red plaid tablecloths on the tables. She had to shoo the flies away with an old church fan. B. J. noticed Mrs. Hattie at the table and hastily sat the iron pot down. Eagerly wanting to do something else, B. J. walked over to Mrs. Hattie and whispered, "Do you need anything else done?" Mrs. Hattie did not seem to hear B.J., as she paused, put her hand under her chin and said, "hum, uh, oh, let me see. Oh, Sonny boy, yoes can gat me dem matches on the shelf in the pantry hean."

A smile crossed his face as he said, "yes, ma'am." Like a flash, B. J. was dashing toward the house. He ignored Mary Jo standing by the tree. He ran up the steps two at a time, whistling a cowboy song.

Momentarily, B. J. was really enjoying himself as he went to the pantry, but he soon realized that Mary Jo was not through with him yet. Suddenly, B. J. had goose bumps running up and down his arms, as he remembered Mary Jo's threat. He mentally got angry with himself and thought "I am going to be smart this time. I am not getting too close to her."

Once he found the matches, B. J. hurried back outside. He was out of breath saying 'Whew! Pooh! Here are the matches Mrs. Hattie. Can I make the fire for you?" Mrs. Hattie already knew that B. J. knew how to make a fire. As a matter of fact, all members of the gang, except the twins, could make a fire.

Mrs. Hattie was so delighted that B. J. offered to help, she let him know he was a big help to her. Mary Jo continued to act mad, and Mrs. Hattie could not use her with that attitude at that moment. "Yoes a big help Sonny boy" Mrs. Hattie said again.

Immediately, B. J. looked around the yard for some twigs to start the fire. Once the fire begins to burn, he can put pieces of charcoal on the fire. Daring not to get too close to Mary Jo, B.J. purposely picked up some twigs, avoiding her look of disapproval.

B.J. deliberately invaded Mary Jo's space. His nonchalant demeanor infuriated an already angry Mary Jo. She defiantly put her hand on hips, positioning herself in the pathway of B.J. She continued her incessant taunting behavior. He quickly turned and instinctively walked over to where Mrs. Hattie was gathering newspapers for the fire.

Staying close to Mrs. Hattie, B.J. pretended to be reading something interesting in the old newspaper. Nervously, B. J. peeped over the paper and observed Mary Jo walking slowly. She had her hand on her forehead as she went up on the porch. *At last*, B. J. thought. *That meddlesome, hot breathed, lizard-eyed girl is leaving me alone.* B. J. laughed, as he hurried to make the fire.

Mary Jo pompously walked up the steps and sat down on the banister. She angrily stared at her mama and B. J., as they were having a conversation, she was not a part of. Feeling left out and with tears welling in her eyes, Mary Jo sadly sulked. With her hands under her chin, Mary Jo enviously said, "Huh, my mama is acting as if B.J. is her child instead of me." Then, she got up from the banister and flopped down in the swing.

Meanwhile, B.J. was tossing pieces of charcoal in the fire While asking, "Mrs. Hattie, is that enough?"

"Shore is Sonny boy," Mrs. Hattie replied. "It is just right for my big skillet over there on dat table."

B.J. was getting excited about the fish fry for Billy Ray again. Having been harassed so much by Mary Jo this morning and afternoon, B. J. had not thought about the fish fry. A sparkle of hope and gladness filled his being as he said, "Yeah, the fish fry." He had forgotten about it, because Mary Jo was really being downright nasty.

The cool breeze was blowing, making a 'wooing' sound as it was rippling through the trees. "De good Lord shore, noes I"s needs dat good air, Sonny boy" Mrs. Hattie said, as she continued to fan.

CHAPTER XXIX
MARY JO BIG SCARE

Everything was peaceful and quiet, as B. J. and Mrs. Hattie finished preparing for the big fish fry, but fate has a way of making us face reality. Things do not necessarily have to stay the way we feel or think they should be. Not even a 'stones, throw away,' fate was about to change. Suddenly, a loud shriek came from the porch. Mrs. Hattie, nervous and alarmed, jumped up from the table and ran over to the porch.

"Mama, Mama, Mama!" Mary Jo shouted out. "I told you Tom was trying to kill me. I was going to sleep on the swing. Then I felt something jump on my chest and something hairy in my face."

"And" Mary Jo said, as she choked a little from talking so fast, "I could smell his stinking breath smelling like old dead fish. And Mama, Tom almost kissed me."

She started pounding her little chubby fist in her hand, saying, "I got him good this time though. He won't be jumping on me or anybody else anymore." Mary Jo said with vengeance.

Mary Jo was acting as if she was telling a story she saw at the movie. She enjoyed telling us every detail of what went on with her and Tom. She was moving from side to side with her hand still beating in the palm of her hand.

For sure, this girl has had too much sun and Tom just set the scenic plot for her. "Then I socked Tom so hard that I knocked him to the floor."

"See, see, Mama, there is Tom," Mary Jo said, as she pointed to the porch floor. Mary Jo was slapping her hands together saying, "I bet you Tom, will think before he tries anything with me from now on, huh?"

B.J. ran up the steps and onto the porch. He was there just in time to see a squirrel leap over the banister. The poor thing ran up the big oak tree. B. J. and Mrs. Hattie tried to hold their composure, but this was too much for them.

It was not Tom but a squirrel. They laughed until tears were rolling down their cheeks. The tears were lapping under their chin. They both had to hold their painful stomachs, but Mary Jo did not think it was that funny.

Finally, Mrs. Hattie said, "Girl, yoes ought not bes so scared of God's creatures. Dat was just a little old squirrel, Mary Jo." Her mama tried not to laugh at her anymore. "Dat squirrel was not going to kill yoe, baby. He probably looking for something to eat. Dat all, baby. Now yoes gat yore self together fore de men comes hean." Mrs. Hattie reached over gingerly and continued, "Yoes noes when the men folk come hean, baby?"

B.J. was beside himself as he went around the house to finish laughing. He was muttering and moaning as he lay out in the dirt. "Good for her," B. J. said aloud as he looked up to the sky. "She has been harassing, annoying and trying to kill me all day with those eyes of hers. Who is she going to bother now? The squirrel." B.J. laughed uncontrollably until it hurt.

Taking his tear-stained glasses off, B.J. wiped his red eyes on his T-shirt. Then he got up from the dirt and dusted his pants off. He proudly strolled around the house as if he was the king now. He held his head high and glanced at Mary Jo, who was giving him the look again.

B.J. did not care anymore. He was not running from her threats. Mary Jo was 'madder than a wet hen.' Now is his time to shine, as if he just won a prizefight. B. J. has had enough of her antagonizing behavior. He just wanted to get a little rest before the railroad men came. It was peaceful now, as he looked around for a cool spot. The big oak tree limbs shaded the steps going up to the porch. He took a seat on the last step and leaned back with his head on the next step. The sun sprinkled down through the big tree.

The surrounding sounds of summer cradled his thoughts. B.J. could feel the settled peace brought on by the rising heat. He was about to drift off to a state of sweet bliss. All was quiet and serene now as B.J. set with his head on the steps. He was gazing at the sunlight sparkling like a diamond through the tree limbs. His spirit was lifted and with anticipation and gladness in his heart, he was filled with joy.

Without prompting or warning, B.J. reflected on what had happened that afternoon. "Huh!" B. J. thought, "That girl shore knows how to use those eyes of hers." He laughed hilariously and said aloud, "Those looks that girl gives you could kill a cat."

However, this did not bother Mary Jo as she leaned back on the swing. The soft wind was blowing across the porch. This is all Mary Jo dwelled on, finding some peace and quietness.

Mrs. Hattie looked over at the children on the porch and steps sleeping like two little angels. She had to catch herself from the thought of the children being angels. "Its bees a battle with dem chillin all morning and afternoon," she thought to herself.

"Theys needs to bes quiet and enjoy this day dat is rite for de fish fry." She took her fan and continued to shoo the flies away. A softly sang a song, as she rocked back and forth to the sound of her voice. Every now and then, she would go check on the fire and add a little more charcoal. She was thinking there was no need to make another fire. She also checked on the fish and made sure all the ice had not melted. The fish had to be fresh, and the ice kept it from spoiling.

Mrs. Hattie walked over toward the street and looked down to see if she could see anyone. She knew it was not time for the men to come, but just wanted to look. All she could see were the heat waves covering the road. She smiled and went over to her chair to sit down.

It was nice and quiet now. Even Tom found a cool spot to lay down and enjoy the quietness. Mary Jo and Tom were the big troublemakers anyway. It started with both of them. "Huh! hum," Mrs. Hattie thought. Dem chillin are doin a good thing for their friend. Theys were happy getting everything for de fish fry. I nos theys will bes helping me a lot when de men come." Mrs. Hattie leaned back in her chair and closed her eyes feeling the cool breeze softly blowing across her face. Slowly she drifted off to sleep and all you heard were the birds flying in and out of the tree.

CHAPTER XX
THE SUMMER HEAT

"Phew!" B.J. quietly said, feeling the biting sun rays parching the back of his neck. He stood up from the steps then, curiously peeped over the banister. He noticed that the tongue-lasher, Mary Jo, was still asleep on the swing. B. J., wobbling, and weak from the heat, uttered out loud, "Huh! I need to find a cool spot too!"

Immediately after he said that he quickly covered his mouth. He had to muffle the sound to avoid waking up Ms. Tongue-lasher. Anxiously, he looked to see if Sleeping Beauty was still asleep. He needed some peace and quietness. He definitely, at no cost, wanted to disturb her.

While straining over the banister again, he noticed that Mary Jo was fast asleep. *Wow!* B.J. thought as he scanned the porch and observed two rocking chairs that seemed to be perfectly placed out of the sun.

Still being mindful not to awaken Mary Jo, B. J. tiptoed up the squeaky steps. He stopped at every squeak, holding his breath so as not to stir her. It caused his heart to beat fast and fiercely but once his feet were on the porch, he no longer felt the need to be quiet. He was not at all concerned about Mary Jo being asleep now.

Furthermore, B. J. was free to act like one of his favorite cowboys. He walked bow-legged across the wooden, gray-painted porch. He put a hard look on his face like his favorite cowboy. Sticking out his scrawny looking chest, he took his shooting finger and pushed his horned-rim, glasses upon his nose. He eased himself over the chair's arm and leaned back saying, "Ah-, ah-ah-ah," as if he was exhaling all the hot air that Mary Jo had been blowing in his face all day. Undaunted, like a good cowboy, he could now have some peace of mind. He closed his eyes and slowly drifted off to sleep.

These two friends were utilizing this time of quietness, as they slept in the afternoon summer heat. You could hear the hummingbirds, butterflies and bumblebees dancing in and out of the summer flowers. A hush of calmness filled the fresh country air. The sound of the squeaky swing played its part like an instrument in a symphony orchestra.

This time of day made it difficult for Mrs. Hattie to sleep very long. She would nod for a little while and then wake up. She walked over to the table with her fan so she could shoo those pesky flies away. Looking toward the porch, she thought Mary Jo and B. J. looked like two little angels fast asleep. "Lawdy bees!" Mrs. Hattie said as she wiped the sweat from her face. "Now ain't dat just like dem chillins, fussin one minute and friends de next. Um,um,um, shore beats everything."

Once at the table, Mrs. Hattie noticed that all the ice had completely melted. The water began to draw flies like a dead June bug. Mrs. Hattie fussed. "Darn old flies, I's wish deys just leave my stuff along huh!"

She gestured to the wind with the swift waving of her church fan. This caused the flies to scatter from the thawing fish. She picked up the fish pan and poured the cloudy water out into the ditch near the street. Mrs. Hattie said, "If dat do not beat all, dem flies was trying to gat my fish, wors-er than dat old Tom cat, um,um,um."

Feeling a little perturbed, Mrs. Hattie decided to put her special seasoning together. She mixed salt, black pepper, red pepper, dried, chopped garlic, a little grated lemon and some of her secret sauce. That is the reason the railroad men would come to her house for some skillet fried golden winter trout. "Hum, Hum, Hum!" Mrs. Hattie said. "I's can taste it now shore can."

The smell of the fish would make her neighbors three blocks away hungry. They would say, "Mrs. Hattie can shore make a person hungry when they just ate. You can bet her neighbors hurry up to her block wanting some of her golden-brown winter trout, with cha-cha on the side." What made Mrs. Hattie's fish taste so good was the seasoning and her sauce. You can just smell and taste her fish sandwich with each bite. Mrs. Hattie stopped long enough to fan herself and finished preparing each fish. As soon as she hears the men coming, she will wake the children up.

The story in this town was that every woman living here had some kind of secret concoction that could, "make you slap your mama and kick your daddy." It is an idiomatic expression that… blacks used to mean something tasted exceptionally good. It had been a while since Mrs. Hattie had cooked a fish fry but when the word got out, people from miles away were eager to enjoy her well-known fried fish. Today was no exception. Many of the men from the railroad would bring a couple of their buddies. These men alone would buy every single piece of

Mrs. Hattie's fish. They would be greedily looking for more. Looking in the distance, Mrs. Hattie said, "That's the four o'clock special bes coming around de bend in no time."

She turned her head to the side, trying to figure out how many minutes she had left. "Those fish had to be ready before the men get here." She knew it was time to, "gat dem chillin up" to help her. Anticipating the busy afternoon ahead of them, Mrs. Hattie nervously called out in a modulated tone of voice. She did not want to frighten them. "It's time for dem men folk, yore needs to gat up now," Looking to see if the children heard her, she called their names again. The afternoon heat had really made the two children sleep hard. Mrs. Hattie, with her hand on her hips, shook her head. She could not believe those children.

"Now don't dat beat all," she said as she expressed amazement that neither of the children stirred from their deep sleep. Mrs. Hattie put her hands in her apron pocket and said, "Deys de one wantin a fish fry for their friends. Uh! Now, What's dat child's name? Oh! Billy boy, yeah, dat his name. And huh! Deys still sleeping. Well," she said smiling, "Deys really cannot do nothing right now anyway."

While moving the coals around in the pot, Mrs. Hattie noticed that the charcoal in the cement pot was white-hot. She shaded her eyes from the sun, in an attempt to look down at the secluded long dirt road. Lost in the moment, Mrs. Hattie noticed that the heat from the sun had caused the road to look wavy. At the same time, it would give the illusion that a person would think something, or someone was there. It was as if seeing ghost-like figures moving. She was aware of the blistering, sweltering heat waves dancing across the sticky tar road that created mysterious forms.

Anticipating the men coming she muttered, "If any dem folk come now, de fire is ready." Picking up her fan, she sat under the tree away from the fire. She thought, *the heat is goina be bad enough when I's start to fry de fish.*

Perhaps Mrs. Hattie had forgotten the quick and drenching afternoon showers. The showers that seemed to come out of nowhere were forecasted for the afternoon. You could tell when these showers were coming because the rising dust would make the wind almost visible. The wind would carry its particles in the brisk breezes. These showers happen so frequently that people would continue with their day. They would not stop and respond to what had become normal for this time of year. They had come to welcome the rain that always seemed to cool the place down. This would help before the sun came back out. The sun could be even more forceful and intense.

Mrs. Hattie just could not sit still. She watched the circle in the middle of the yard. *Good*, she thought, *it will help cool de place down and a little water don't hurt no one*. Next, a ventilating wind blew brisk air her way, and she gracefully said, "Just what da good Lord ordered. Shore is," as she continued to prepare the table for her soon to be coming guests.

Looking over at the cement pot, Mrs. Hattie realized it was time to put the big iron skillet on the fire. She proceeded to cut the soft lard into two pieces to put one in the skittle. She wrapped the other piece of lard to be used later. Mrs. Hattie would test the temperature of the lard by flipping some water in the hot grease. She watched to see if the water would dance around making sizzling sounds. This was to make sure the grease was just right so the fish would fry golden brown. She knew it was almost time to put the fish in the hot grease. "Hum!" Mrs. Hattie said, as the favor of the frying fish filled the air, making a hound dog want some of her fish.

CHAPTER XXI
HERE COMES THE MEN FOLK

The time had come for the fish to be cooked, while Mary Jo and B. J. were trying to get moving. Both of the children had a long nap and were slowly waking up. Mary Jo's legs weren't acting right, as they were still asleep. She attempted to stand up but fell down again. Meanwhile, the coals in the pot were just how Mrs. Hattie wanted them. She had her poker spread the coals to maintain a uniform heat pattern. Mrs. Hattie could see through the dust down the road. There were unrecognizable figures hastily walking toward the house. "Could dat bes de men folk?" She said to herself with a questioning look on her face. To make certain these were the men folk, she walked closer to the roadside to get a better look.

For a moment, the road had been covered in dust. Then, a big smile came across her face. She rushed over to the porch steps again and yelled, "Mary Jo and B.J., get up, de men folk are coming. Git up, and hurry up, you all needs to come and help me."

Mary Jo blinked, rubbed her eyes, and looked curiously around the porch. Then it hit her like a light bulb. The men must be coming. Her legs felt as if they had pins and needles pricking them still. This made her attempt to stand up fast. She fell down as a result of the numb and lifeless state of her legs. She rubbed her legs vigorously and shaking them until they began to feel normal again.

In the meantime, B. J. began to stir from his nap, looking as if he were lost. His eyes were big and glossy. His glasses were hanging sideways on the edge of his nose. After a couple of unsuccessful attempts, he was able to push them back one his face correctly. He quickly wiped the drool from his face. Wanting to know what happened, he said, "Mary Jo, what's all the noise, huh?"

Mary Jo was still yawning and stretching her arms. She yelled in a sassy snappy manner, "Just get up, B. J. The men folk are coming up the road right now!"

"Uh!" B. J. thinking *that girl is still acting like a grumpy old lady.* He jumped to his feet, thinking that the swiftness of the movement would get his feet and the rest of his body moving.

Carefully, he rubbed and wiggled his bony, bowlegs nonstop, still trying to get back into them. "Sitting in a straight position for a couple of hours must have caused my legs to go to sleep," B.J. said. "Wow!" He said as he stumbled down the steps. "I forgot all about the fish fry."

Approaching the cement pot, B. J. eagerly asked what she wanted him to do. She said, "All right Sonny boy, make sure yoes git how many fish sandwiches the men wants to git."

B.J. was overjoyed to take the men's orders. He was excited as he took a seat at the table. Lying in front of him was a tablet and a pencil. B. J. decided to put numbers down each line on the paper. This will help him keep up with how many sandwiches they sold. *This is a man's job anyways,* B. J. thought. *Because boys have to use numbers all of the time.* He had better be glad that Mary Jo did not know he was thinking such nonsense.

In the meantime, Mary Jo casually walked over to the table where B. J. was busy folding some napkins. She looked to see if her mama was looking her way. She immediately took the opportunity to harass B. J. once more as she gave him the evil eye. This was her way of looking at someone eye to eye when she was still mad at them. She whispered, "I have not forgotten about this morning, B.J. Perkins, Jr. you hear?"

Vaguely remembering the morning's activity, B. J., who was still trying to get the sleep out of his brain, shook his head and acknowledged he remembered. "Un! Huh! Mary Jo, I know," he said.

He never stopped his assignment, as he pounded the napkin he was folding. Realizing she was being ignored, she made a gesture with her hands folded in disgust. She stood, waiting for her mama to tell her what to do. Looking over the table, Mrs. Hattie told Mary Jo, "Go help Sonny boy fold de napkins."

Mary Jo was very annoyed because that was not what she had planned to do. In her usual arrogant manner, she thought, "I have better things to do than fold dumb napkins," and was aggravated with her assignment. *Uh, aha,* Mary Jo thought, as she put on her innocent face and timid voice that resembled a kitten purring. She asked her Mama, "Mama, uh you know them men folk going to be mighty thirsty when they get here. Why don't I make some Kool-Aid and sell it?"

Mrs. Hattie put her hand under her chin, as if to ponder the question before answering her. Mary Jo insistently pleaded, "May I Mama? Ma'am, may I please?" She looked at her mama with her big brown eyes.

Her mama smiled and kindly said, "Yes siree little girl, dat wool bes good. Yoes can git de big tin pitcher in de pantry on the top shelf. I think there's some of dat strawberry kind still left hean! Uh, huh, uh, Hun! Oh! Mary Jo yoes can use dat small block of ice in the icebox too."

This really made Mary Jo's day as she thanked her mama. Mary Jo burst with excitement as she ran into the house shouting. "Oh gosh," she said, as she went into the pantry to get the pitcher off the top shelf. She grabbed a chair from the table and stood up on her tiptoes to reach it.

Mary Joe made the Kool-Aid to taste almost as good as her mamas'. Mrs. Hattie taught her the art of making almost anything taste good. Mary Jo sampled the Kool-Aid by pouring herself a cup full. It tasted just as if her mama made it. "Um, Un!" she said. "That will take all the poison out of it." That was something she had heard her mama say when she sampled what she cooked or made. She picked up the pitcher to take it outside. When she reached the screen door, she pushed it open with her knee and yelled for B.J. to come carry the pitcher over to the table.

B.J. was in another world. He did not hear her when she called him, so he continued to look out into space while folding the napkins. Mrs. Hattie, knowing that B. J. was daydreaming, said, "Sonny boy, Mary Jo need some help with dat pitcher of Kool-Aid all right?"

"Oh, oh, yes ma'am, Mrs. Hattie. I did not hear her calling me." B.J. said. He carefully laid the napkins down and ran over to the steps to help Mary Jo.

"Here B.J.," Mary Jo said, carefully giving him the pitcher of Kool-Aid ordering him not to drop it. B. J., not wanting to get an argument started with her, remained silent.

Suddenly he remembered that she had just said please to him, and he muttered softly, "I wonder if the girl has lost it?" He sheepishly smiled as he hurried back over to the table. B.J. was about to sit down when he noticed the yard was full of railroad men. "Wow!" he said. "Mary Jo, they are here!"

Instantly, she smiled and began to escort the men to a cool spot in the yard. Some of the regular men decided to stand around talking to Mrs. Hattie. B.J. gleefully took each man's order. This happened around the time Mrs. Hattie's grease was just right. She began putting five pieces of fish in the hot grease. Within seconds, the scent of the frying fish filled the air. The smell was so pungent, that it stimulated the senses. One man said, "Ah, um-mm!" as if he could taste the fish already.

Mary Jo was sauntering around with her nose in the air. She smiled as she proudly sold her Kool-Aid for five cents a glass. B. J. was collecting dollar bills, half dollars, nickels, dimes, and even some pennies. He took each man's money and put it into the sack. He was pretending that he was an important businessman. Mrs. Hattie began to sing a church song, while some of the men ate their sandwiches, hollering at each other not to bother Mrs. Hattie about another sandwich. "Eat the one you got Joe. Stop pestering Mrs. Hattie," one man said.

CHAPTER XXII
THE FISH FRY

As fast as Mrs. Hattie could get a batch of fish cooked, the men, who were voraciously indulging themselves, would say to the others, "Do not point your finger at me and use up all of Mrs. Hattie's chow-chow." Chow-chow is a type of garnish used in the South.

You could hear another man say, "This is the best fish in town," as he asked for another sandwich. Mrs. Hattie was cooking as fast as she could but noticed her fire was dying. She quickly reached for the charcoal bag but found it empty.

"Sonny boy," Mrs. Hattie called out, "goes around to the shed and bring me dat bag of charcoal, please."

B.J. happily ran around the house to the shed. Once inside, he quickly grabbed the charcoal and ran toward the front yard. He was not paying any attention to anything other than resting. Having rested, he thought it was time for him to play with whoever or whomever happened to come his way. B.J. was about to approach the spot where Tom was hiding. This cat was about to make his move and B.J. was unaware of the incident that was about to take place. Tom had positioned himself on the windowsill in a tiger-like leaping position as if he were waiting to pounce upon his prey. His head was erect like a grotesque evil statue that was about to come alive and catch someone off guard.

Tom successfully leaped at B. J.'s chest. After accomplishing his heroic feat, he held on. This scared B. J. so badly that he let out a piercing squeal that could have awakened the entire neighborhood. Terrified, he took off running as if he was in a marathon heading towards the front yard and instantly dropped the bag of charcoal. The men jumped up to see what all the commotion was. They noticed B.J. running and trying to get Tom off his chest. Tom had locked his claws into B. J.'s shirt. The men folk, Mrs. Hattie, and Mary Jo could not do anything but laugh and repeatedly say, "Tom, stop it!"

When B. J. stopped sprinting, old Tom jumped down and ran under the table. B.J. was angry and embarrassed by what just happened. Being self-conscious, he looked over at Mary Jo. She was laughing so hard that she was twisting her body and hurried to the bathroom.

It was not that funny to B. J. However, he thought about how insensitive Mary Jo was behaving. After all, that cat could make a person hurt themselves. He also thought about how Mary Jo must have felt earlier. Feeling a sense of remorse, B. J. walked at a snail's pace back to the table and flopped down in the chair. Mrs. Hattie went over to check on him to make sure Tom did not hurt him. B. J. was more embarrassed than anything that he screamed as if he was a little girl. Mary Jo is never going to let him forget what happened today. You can bet on that and the loud noises he was making.

B.J. could not have known that Tom would do something of that nature. He acted as bad as a person walking up behind you and frightened you. This was an unexpected situation, so B. J. responded by yelling as if someone was killing him. Even Mary Jo seemed to be reconsidering what Tom did to her. She does not have that scornful look on her face anymore.

Nevertheless, both of the children have learned a good lesson. Fate has a way of surprising all of us. It is up to each person to decide how they will accept it. Mary Jo could feel and sense how B. J. was feeling. She knew now that he was really sorry for not stopping Tom from attacking her. This was his mindset at that time not knowing that something could happen to him too. Looking back, he now understands the embarrassment and hurt pride when people are making fun of you, when it is not funny to the person who is being attacked.

Mary Jo came down off her high horse to show B. J. compassion. With all the men folk around laughing, B. J. was trying to act as if he was a man, but he was just a little kid that needed their help. What a day this has been from one adventure after another, all because of a cat named Tom. B.J. told Mary Jo how sorry he was.

Mrs. Hattie noticed the children as they rekindled their friendship. They needed to continue helping Mrs. Hattie and Mary Jo needed to get the men to buy her Kool-Aid. It was time to get back to the reason for the fish fry. This was a happy time, as Mrs. Hattie smiled at the children being friends again. She continued to fry up a batch of fish for the men folk. The railroad men seemed not to get enough of her golden-brown fish. They all stood around like hungry bears up a tree after some honey. They were all talking and laughing about who was going to get the next pieces of fish.

Mary Jo did not seem to mind all the fuss that the men were doing. She just hoped that every piece of fish would be sold. Her thought was to make enough money for Billy Ray's gift. Mary Jo and B. J. were doing a good job making sure the men had enough. There was peace now as B. J. and Mary Jo realized that some things are not as funny as one may think.

In the meantime, Mary Jo and B. J. were back on their job helping the men. She was happy and continued to sell her Kool-Aid to the men. B. J. wanted a glass of Kool-Aid but thought it was best to leave it alone since he was now on her good side, and this is where he wanted to be. He continued his job, going around collecting money for fish sandwiches. Mrs. Hattie was gleaning all over as she looked at the children and how well they were behaving. She noticed Mary Jo giving B. J. the money from a man who just bought two fish sandwiches. Things were looking up for the kids, learning how to take care of business.

They want to buy their friend a nice gift. They had been at this all day, from the alley hunt, going, taking their findings to the iron works to get the money to go shopping and going to the store. They were indeed true friends that went beyond what a grown-up might do.

Mrs. Hattie was so proud of B. J. and Mary Jo for finally working together to buy their friend a nice gift. She laughed at the trouble they were having this morning with each other. She thought *that child of mine is so bossy. She is always trying to be somebody's mama.* She smiled and finished taking the last pieces of fish out of the frying pan thinking, *there are still hungry men to feed.* Then, she remembered to save two nice pieces for B.J. and Mary Jo. After all, this was their fish fry, and they earned a right to enjoy some of their labor. Mrs. Hattie called the children and told them to take a seat. She brought each of them a nice big fish laid out on two pieces of bread.

Their eyes lit up as they looked down at the big golden-brown piece of fish. They each put hot sauce, chow-chow and a little salt on their sandwiches. They sat down at the table while Mrs. Hattie gave each of them a cold glass of Mary Jo's Kool-Aid. Mary Jo and B. J. were happy as they sat and enjoyed the summer day. B. J, was excited, thinking about how much money they made, but he did not want to upset Mary Jo. He was too busy eating his fish sandwich and making sure to spit out the bones. If they did get a bone caught in their throat, Mrs. Hattie had a cure for that too. She would give them a piece of cornbread and that would make the bone go down. The children seem to be doing alright. They were laughing, eating and enjoying their togetherness.

Mrs. Hattie was sitting at the table talking to the men folk that comes around every time they have a layover in Johnson City. She is talked about down through the railroad towns. These men would put the word out that her yard was the best place in town to buy her golden-brown fish sandwiches.

The children will be happy to know that every man brought two or three fish sandwiches. She had saved two fish for the children. It seemed as if they did a good job with sales from the fish fry and Kool-Aid, plus two extra dollars that a man gave Mary Jo.

Some of the men were just hanging around in Mrs. Hattie's yard. Mostly talking about the different cities, they have traveled to. B.J. liked to hear about other cities that these men had traveled to. He would ask the men about the flowers, bugs, and whether the ocean was blue like the pictures on the postcards.

Mary Jo was not interested in what B.J. was talking about. She went over and sat on the porch steps and enjoyed the twilight, while the lightning bugs put on a show lighting up the night. The moths had their part in this show as they circled around the porch light. B.J. took a seat beside Mary Jo and said he was so sorry for not helping her, again. She reached out to tell him it was alright. "We got the job done today. Now! We can get Billy Ray a nice gift; something he can remember us by and enjoy for a long time." she said, getting teary eyed, but she quickly wiped the tears away before B.J. saw it.

She did not want to be sad, but the time to be happy for Billy Ray. B. J. and Mary Jo did not have any sisters or brothers; they both were only children. It is different when there are more than two children in the house, like Billy Ray has. Mary Jo's mama cooks for her as if there were five children in the house. B. J.'s mama does him the same way. How blessed both of them are.

"This truly a good day to help dem chillinn have a fish fry for their friend. "Un! dat shore was nice of dem chillin to think about doin something special for a friend." She smiled, as she began to take the tablecloths off of the table. She put them in her Maytag washing machine, which was sitting on the back porch. She did want that fish smell smelling up her house. Sometimes it takes days to get rid of that smell out of a house.

Mary Jo and B. J. noticed Mrs. Hattie and the handyman, cleaning up everything. They were too tired to help. Mrs. Hattie did not bother them because they worked hard all day. She decided that they would count the money later.

B.J's main concern now was the money. He did not fool Mary Jo because she knew that is all this boy had talked about all day. He wanted to know. She said, "B.J., we will count the money later, Ok?"

"Well, uh ah, uh," B.J. said, stumbling over his words and not knowing what to say.

Mary Jo being contentious said, "B. J., Tom scared all the sense out of you? What do you mean? 'Uh, ah, uh?' You beginning to act like Billy Ray with that, 'uh, ah, uh.' I do not", as she put her finger on the tip of his nose. "What do you mean?"

"Oh no, Mary Jo," B. J., quickly responded, "I was just wondering how much money you made off the Kool- Aid." B. J. smirked, as he waited for Mary Jo to answer him.

"Oh!" Mary Jo quickly said. "I forgot all about the money because we were working so hard, B. J."

Nonetheless, she started teasing B. J. as she stood up. She reached into her pocket and pulled out all dimes, nickels, quarters, and pennies. He anxiously looked and wondered how much money they had made. "How much money Jo? Huh, huh, huh?"

Being self-important, she ignored B. J., as she took her time and counted the money. Mary Jo was pleasantly surprised that she had made four dollars and five cents. Counting the two-dollar bills that one of the men from the railroad gave her, it came up to six dollars and five cents. "Gosh lee! That is a whole lot of money, B. J." Mary Jo eagerly said.

"We are rich-h-h-h!" B.J. said in a squeaky voice. "And, and just think of all the things we can do and buy now." At the same time, he was wondering how much money they made from the fish fry. This was more important than her little Kool-Aid sale. B.J. was thinking he put a whole lot of dollars in that happy sack. All B.J. was interested in was how much money they had made in total.

CHAPTER XXIII
HOW MUCH MONEY DID WE MAKE?

Mrs. Hattie heard the happy sounds from the children and walked over to the table. She sensed that they wanted to be by themselves, as she approached the table. They had a big job to do; count the money from the fish fry.

Earlier, B. J. gave Mrs. Hattie the sack to hold. She said, "Hean, Mary Jo and Sonny boy, dis is de money from the fish fry."

B.J. eyes got as big as the lens in his glasses. He looked at the little sack with all the money bulging out. Spontaneously Mrs. Hattie laughed and said, "yoes chillin, did well today. Shore did, huh?"

Mary Jo quickly took the little sack and said, "B.J., we need to wait until we help Mama and Mr. Leroy. You know the yard needs cleaning up." B. J. did not want to wait till later. His brain was already trying to figure out how much money they made.

He agreed to help her take the paper napkins, glasses, and the tin pitcher to the kitchen. Looking strangely at B.J., Mary Jo said, "you know B.J., we need to give Mama half of the money. After all, she's the one that came up with the idea. She did most of the work too."

B.J. paused and contemplated his decision about the money. His attention was focused on the unselfish act Mary Jo was initiating. He thought, "when, does she think about anyone but herself?" The answer to the question was a source of serious concern for him.

"Well, uh!" B, J, finally said, as he peeped over his glasses. "I think that is a swell idea, Mary Jo. How much do you say you want to give your mama?"

Mary Jo stared right into his big eyes and said, "look, B.J. Perkins Jr., half. Can you count, half, ok?" She was nervously thinking that B.J. might not agree with her.

Unremoved by her outburst, B.J. casually said, "Yeah, Mary Jo, I guess that will be alright." He sat down at the table. He was trying not to show that he did not really agree. Mary Jo wanted to do too much with the proceeds from the fish fry. He thought again, almost saying too loud, "Mrs. Hattie was supposed to be helping us out."

After all, her mama did not give us one red cent. We had to go look for scrap iron, pop bottles and rags. B. J. was thinking about how they did not make that much from selling the items.

"If it had not been for the good Lord putting that money where Mary Jo could find it, we would not have enough for the things we needed." He emphasized what he was saying as if he was frustrated. Disappointed with the assumption Mary Jo had made, he shook his head and sulked.

Mary Jo got up from the table and said, "let's go back outside, B. J." Once outside, he noticed how quickly the sun had gone down. The evening breeze had brought a refreshing aroma that scented the air. The day was drawing its final scene. The night creatures were ready, and the little people had accomplished what they had set their little minds to do that day.

"Gee whiz!" B. J. excitedly said, as the air seemed to clear his senses, "I cannot wait until tomorrow." This has been one heck of a day. It was well spent; no time wasted. These two little people showed how much love they had for their friend, Billy Ray.

Sighing, Mary Jo sat down on the porch with B. J. sitting across from her. They counted the money. Without any preliminaries, a big smile came across B. J.'s face. He carefully said, "Billy Ray is going to be soooo happy, Mary Jo. We can buy him something big, Huh, huh huh!?"

"Yeah," she softly said, "But what, B. J.? What can we buy him that is big huh?"

"Maybe your mama can give us some good ideas, Mary Jo," B. J. said with a little reservation.

Mrs. Hattie was sitting in the swing at the other end of the porch. She was concerned about whether they made enough for the gift. She was thinking about telling the children if they had not made enough, they could do another fish fry.

The children did not have to go looking for something to sell this time. They could use some of the money that they have made. Mrs. Hattie thought of ideas, just in case. "That will be the solution to what they may need." She let out a sigh of relief, as she noticed the children coming towards her. Mrs. Hattie decided to wait before she asked Mary Jo how much they made.

Mary Jo walked over to her mama with compassion in her voice Mary Jo said, "Mama, Mama, we made twenty- dollars off of the fish fry. The Kool-Aid sale we made four dollars and five cents."

She did not mention the two-dollar bill that one of the men from the railroad had given her. Looking at B.J. with her look, he knew not to say anything about the money either. Those eyes of hers are something else. They keep that little gang of hers in control. She had plans for that two-dollar bill and after all, it was hers to keep. She planned to share it with her friends.

In the meantime, Mrs. Hattie was overjoyed with how much the children made from the fish fry. She told Mary Jo that they could buy Billy Ray a nice gift. "Dat is so nice of you and Sonny boy to think about your friend first."

B. J. was really in the moment, as he stuck out his little chest acting like his favorite cowboy. Then B.J. quickly spoke up and said "yes, ma'am, Mrs. Hattie after we give you your money first, fair and square. You helped Mary Jo and me so much. We could not have done it without you. Here, Mrs. Hattie, we want you to have half of the money."

Listening on the sidelines, Mary Jo could not believe what B. J. had just had the nerve to do. "Just thirty minutes prior, he was against giving my mama half of the money. He must have gotten struck by some lightning."

"Now he is playing the role of the good guy. Wow! What a guy. Just listen to him trying to act as if he came up with the idea." She did not want to make him feel uncomfortable or burst his big bubble, so she decided not to tell.

Mary Jo let B. J. take all the credit for being unselfish and thoughtful, even though he did not come up with an initial idea of how to make the money for Billy Ray's gift. It was Mary Jo's, Mama, who told her what they could do.

It was time for Mary Jo to shine as she said, "Yes ma'am and you worked so hard for us today. We appreciated all the things that you put into making this fish fry the best ever."

This was B. J.'s time, to listen to what Mary Jo had to say about what her mama did for them. B.J. had his leg apart, standing like a cowboy with the little chest pumped out, and his hand under his chin with his mouth twisted. All this kid needed now were two guns hanging off his bony hips. Mrs. Hattie looked over at B. J. and laughed thinking if a gust of wind blew, it would blow him right off the porch.

Nevertheless, Mary Jo continued to give her mama the praise that she deserved. She was back on her soapbox trying to be the drama queen. B. J. was so frustrated that he had to grit his teeth, to keep from saying anything. He thought, *just as soon as we are out of Mrs. Hattie's sight, I am going to give her the what fors. I am going to tell her a few things and take that crown right off her head.*

Mrs. Hattie laughed and thanked the children for the money but, to their surprise, she only took six dollars. She suggested that they buy Billy Boy a cowboy outfit. They knew that Billy Ray loved cowboys. Wow!" B. J. and Mary Jo said at the same time. "That is it! We can buy Billy Ray a cowboy outfit."

"Yes ma'am, Mary Jo," her mama said. "You can git him one of those outfits at Park's department store downtown."

"Really, Mama?" Mary Jo said. "We have enough for a whole outfit!"

"Shore nough, little girl," Mrs. Hattie said. "Yoes could git him…." She paused and then asked B. J. and Mary Jo, "What is dat cowboy's name dat Billy Ray like?"

"Oh!" Mrs. Hattie said. "Git him dat." She laughed and said again, "Dat goina bes one happy boy. He got some special friends to buy him a gift like dat, uh, hun," as she continued to swing.

CHAPTER XXIV
B. J.'S OVERNIGHT STAY AT MARY JO'S HOUSE

Since it was getting late Mrs. Hattie said, "Sonny boy, yoes can spend the night. Mr. Bill is in Chicago and won't be back till next week. Yoes can sleep in his room."

B. J. was all smiles as he said, "You mean I can stay the night?"

"Yessiree," Mrs. Hattie said. "Mr. Leroy is cleaning things up in the yard. When he finishes, I'll git him to run over to yore house and let yore mama know. It is getting late, and you all worked hard today. Yose need to spend the night. In the morning after breakfast, I's send yose home, all right B. J.?"

B. J. was so pleased that he did not have to walk home. He did not realize how tired he was until he stood up. His back was stiff, and his arms were sore. All he wanted now was a bed to fall into. He could not believe what the day had brought him. Now, it was ending with the joy of finally spending the night at Mrs. Hattie's house. B. J. had a big smile on his face. This boy was in seventh heaven.

On the other hand, Mary Jo was too tired to be concerned over B. J.'s fate. She was thinking about going upstairs and getting into her bed. As she stood at the bottom stairwell looking up, she dreaded climbing all of those stairs, but B. J. was euphoric and on cloud nine. He climbed the stairs and waited for Mary Jo to come up. The sour looks on her face definitely showed that she was not in the mood. She did not want to be bothered with B. J. She hurriedly walked up the stairs giving him a blank, detached look. B. J. knew Mary Jo was tired because he was out of it himself.

"Well, B. J." Mary Jo said as she felt a little weak from the long day's work. "What is it you want?"

He had a big smile on his face and happily said, "Thank you, Mary Jo, for letting me spend the night. You know I rarely get to spend the night at anyone's house. This is a no-no with my mama. She would always tell me she needs me at home. You know, Mary Jo, she still thinks I am her baby."

B.J.'s mama knew what she was doing because some people's houses weren't the best places to spend the night.

Mary Jo thought, *I do not want to know the history of his life.* All she wanted right then was her bed, but to appease B.J., Mary Jo said, "B.J., maybe it is because your mama loves you."

Mary Jo was holding her head as if it was hurting her badly. This did not phase B.J., as he did not respond to her actions. Finally, B. J. answered, "I guess so, Mary Jo. My mama Do love me."

He continued leaning on the handrail. He was hoping she would walk him down the dimly lit hallway. B. J. was too uptight to ask a girl to walk him to his room, knowing Mary Jo probably would not let him live it down.

Mary Jo, annoyed and still holding on to the banister, finally said, "B.J., go to bed. I will talk to you in the morning. Ok?"

B.J. not really wanting to respond said, "Oh, all right Mary Jo. Goodnight."

Having gotten over his initial fear, B. J. anxiously walked down the hallway to Mr. Bill's room. Once at the door he curiously looked around as if he thought he would see someone. He hurried into the room and grabbed the long string to turn on the light that hung in the middle of the ceiling. He was stunned as he looked around the room. He thought, *why was I so afraid? Mr. Bill's room is spotless.* There was not a book, an article of clothing, shoes, paper, or anything out of its place.

B.J. said, "Wow!" His room was scarier than this one. Unlike this room, his room is cluttered with different kinds of bugs, frogs, and anything else that crawled, lived in water, or flew about. B.J. used most of his bedroom as a lab and nothing else. Scanning the room as if it were an X-ray machine, B. J. excitedly observed some rare stamps in a glass frame sitting on the dresser. He saw odd-looking figures on a shelf in the corner.

He walked over to a corner, where there were many books, maps, pins, and other things that brought excitement to his adventurous mind. The room was filled with items Mr. Bill had brought home from his numerous travels on the train. B.J. was in awe, as he took a closer look at the beautiful butterfly collection in a wooden glass frame that hung on the wall. Near Mr. Bill's chair was a magazine rack that held the National Geographic, Ebony, Time, The Chicago Defender, and various other books. Finally, he sat down on the bed and said, "Wow! Billy Ray is not going to believe that Mr. Bill has all of these things." Suddenly, he jumped when he heard a soft knock at his door. "Come in," he said.

"Sonny boy, it's me," Mrs. Hattie said as she entered the room and handed him the shirt. "Yoes hurry and git in the bed. Hean yoe are Sonny boy! Yoes git into bed cause I noes yoes is tired from all dat work today." After that, she leaned over and kissed him on the forehead. "Goodnight Sonny boy," she said, as she turned to leave the room.

B. J. responded, "Good night Mrs. Hattie. Thank you for letting me spend the night."

Mrs. Hattie left the room and softly closed the door.

B. J. was not impressed with the nightshirt, since he thought it looked like a girl's gown. He hastily took off his clothes and neatly laid them across the arm of the chair. After putting the nightshirt on, he looked at himself in the old, mahogany, floor mirror and said, "Ugh! This is a girl's nightshirt."

Yawing, B. J. reached up, grabbed the string again to turn the light off, and jumped into the bed. He could feel the coolness of the starched and ironed sheets as he peacefully drifted off to sleep.

Before Mrs. Hattie went to bed, she walked down the hallway to check on "Sonny boy." She tipped-toed quietly into the room, peeped over at the bed, noticed him fast asleep and said, "Now ain't dat precious, sleeping like an angel."

Then she gently closed the door and went to her room. She hurried and took off her shoes, thinking, *this shore has been a busy day, full of things happening wit dat child of mine.* "Uh!"

Mary Jo was fast asleep, as Mrs. Hattie slowly eased into the big bed. She was tired too, as she laid there placidly thinking about the big events that went on earlier that day. She laughed as she thought about Mary Jo and Tom, Tom and B. J. and dat poor old squirrel that Mary Jo knocked to the floor. She "knew dat was Tom she was getting back at."

By this time, tears were streaming down her face as she muffled her laughter. She did not want to wake the children up. She thought *Mr. Bill is not goina believe what has happened today.* He's goina think I's makin dis up. Uh ,uh shore is," as she answered herself. Mrs. Hattie stopped herself from thinking about the day. Fluffing up her pillows, she turned over on her right side and went to sleep.

CHAPTER XXV
FRIENDS FOREVER ENJOYING THE QUIETNESS OF SHARING

B. J. and Billy Ray usually dreaded the long walk to Mary Jo's house, but today was special. They did not mind the stuffy air or the heat from the sun bearing down on their faces. Mary Jo had promised the gang a treat at the picture show. Billy Ray was especially anxious to get there because a new movie was playing today. His favorite cowboy, Hop-Along-Cassidy, was starring in *War Wagon.*

Wow! What a treat! he thought. The more he thought about it, the more excited he became. Billy Ray was not worried about the heat now. He just wanted to get there before this girl changed her mind because she had to wait for us. This was all Billy Ray needed so he put some pep in his step. He was walking so fast that B. J. had to run to keep up with him. Billy Ray was so engrossed in his thoughts about the movie that he completely left B.J. behind.

B.J. had to stop several times to catch his breath. He yelled out, "Hey! Bill Ray, wait for me."

He immediately turned and noticed how far behind B. J. was. Billy Ray said, "Come on slowpoke, we do not want to miss the show." He waved his hand for him to hurry up.

B. J. said, "I am coming, just wait right there." Billy Ray took the opportunity to find some shade to sit down. He decided to rest under a tree by the road, until B.J. could catch up. Every now and then a cool breath of air would blow his way. "Ah-h-h-h," he would say as the air felt good to his now sweaty face.

Finally, B. J. ran up saying, "Woo-woo!" as he flopped down next to Billy Ray on the damp grass. "It is too hot to do anything but sit on Mary Jo's porch and drink some Kool-Aid, huh, Billy Ray?"

"Uh! That would be kind of nice, but we're going to the show, remember?" Billy Ray replied. Billy Ray, playing with a blade of grass, said, "B. J., did you forget about the black hawk cherry tree?"

"Whoa, whoa, let me tell you," B. J. said, as he stood up. Looking down at Billy Ray, he said, "Mary Jo won't let me forget because every time she is around all she talks about is her grabby fingers."

They looked at each other and burst out laughing. "That girl is something to be tied-up with, huh, Billy Ray?" B. J. said, as he sat back down.

The boys laid under the tree without saying anything for a while. "Billy Ray," B. J. said. "I was reminiscing about the good times the gang had." He had a deep yearning to tell Billy Ray about the fish fry, but he needed to keep it to himself. After all, he would have to deal with Mary Jo, and it was not worth listening to her mouth.

In that moment, two boys enjoyed the quietness of sharing unspoken memories. B. J. sat wrapped deep in his thoughts, playing them over in his mind. It was like looking through a picture album, while Billy Ray sat motionless, locked in a daydream. To break the silence, B. J., lying back in the grass with his hands under his head, excitedly said, "Guess what, Billy Ray?"

"What, B. J.?" Billy Ray quickly replied.

"Mudear is taking me shopping to get me some new clothes for school next week." B. J. said.

Billy Ray, not sounding too enthused about B.J.'s happy news replied, "I bet you get those corduroy knickers you want Huh! B.J."

"Yeah!" B. J. said, getting up off the ground looking down at Billy Ray.

"Maybe B. J.," Billy Ray said, "you will get a pair of penny loafers too."

He really wanted some penny loafers instead of those Buster Brown's shoes you can never wear out. "They are for babies anyway, not for boys like me," B.J. thought. "We are going to be getting out of this school before we know it." Reaching into his back pocket, B.J. took out a tobacco sack.

Billy Ray asked B. J., "What is that for? Huh!"

B. J. reached in the sack and took out two shiny pennies, but Billy Ray still did not understand. B. J. told Billy Ray "These two shiny pennies are to put in my new penny loafers."

Billy Ray said, "That is so right," as he hit his forehead for not knowing what the pennies meant. Billy Ray knew that B.J. loved eating strawberry kits all of the time too. He figured that was why he had the two pennies. Billy Ray let B. J. know how nice they are going to look in his new loafers.

Thinking about what was going to happen in the next few days, B. J. had a big lump in his throat that felt as if it was a giant boulder. B. J. managed to tell Billy Ray he was like a brother to him and that he loved him. In that instant, the boys began to cry so hard that they were acting as if they were two babies that needed their dirty diapers changed. What a sight to see out in the hot sun. Standing by the roadside were these two boys crying, as their hearts were breaking. In the midst of the tears, the boys looked at each other and burst out laughing.

At last Billy Ray could talk as he said, "Silly me B. J."

"Yea, ah, Billy Ray I think both of us were pretty silly."

Billy Ray pointed his finger and said, "You should have seen that ugly face, and with your turned up lips crying like a baby wanting a bottle B. J." Billy Ray continued, "That is just the half of it my friend, you were crying so much that your eyes are like them old men down at the Juke Joint drinking Moonshine"

"Both of our eyes are fiery red, and Mary Jo will say we have been swimming or crying for them to get that red." B.J. responded.

Surprised by what B. J. said, Billy Ray quickly responded, "No kidding B. J. Wow! I cannot go over to Mary Jo's house looking like this." He tried to wipe the red off his eyes with the end of his T–shirt. Billy Ray just made matters worse. His eyes were still reddish looking.

Billy Ray said, "We can walk slower, B. J.," as he picked up a rock and tossed it.

"Uh Hun! Uh! Hun! Shore can Billy Ray," B. J. said, as they leisurely walked down the road again. As Billy Ray and B.J. were walking, something strange occurred. A Blue Jay sat on B. J.'s shoulder.

"Look, look!" Billy Ray said ecstatically. "It is not flying away! It is not flying away!" Billy Ray was flabbergasted, as he shook his head in disbelief. This was too good to be true. He thought, *well at least it is not one of his favorite pets, snakes.* Billy Ray squelched at the sound of the word snakes. The slithering thing made his skin itch and his stomach queasy.

Nevertheless, the old nature boy seemed to draw all sorts of creatures. These creatures around the town seemed to know when B. J. is around. Billy Ray, still dumbfounded, asked, "B. J., do you know this bird or something huh, huh?" At that moment, Billy Ray was talking to himself because B. J. is so engrossed in what he is doing that he did not hear Billy Ray. "B. J., B. J.," Billy Ray yelled out, "it is getting hot out here." Billy Ray had enough of B. J. and that silly bird. They have wasted enough time. It was time to go, and he knows how Mary Jo does not like to wait.

"Let the dumb bird go so we can get to Mary Jo's house." Billy Ray said.

B. J. was now acting as if he was in a daze. Slowly saying, "Ok, ok." He gently tapped the bird on the tail, and it flew away. "Golly Gee!" B. J. said, enthusiastically. "Billy Ray, did you see that? Huh!"

At this point, Billy Ray let B. J. know he had eyes, and he could see what that dumb bird did. Billy Ray wanted to know if he knew the bird's mama or something. B. J., looking bewildered softly, said, "No." Actually, that was his first encounter with any bird. It was strange but strange things happen when we least expect it.

Billy Ray, still in a mood, sarcastically said, "You could have fooled me." He changed the subject and wanted to know if B.J. was going to work with animals when he was grown.

The intellectual side of B.J. began to sprout out, as he explained to Billy Ray that he was going to be a scientist. "Aha!" Billy Ray said, "That's why you are so smart, huh B.J.?"

B. J. let Billy Ray know that "Everybody is born with knowing something that someone else does not know how to do. You need to discover what it is?" Billy Ray's eyes lit up and he had a big smile on his face. His friend made him feel that he could be whatever he wanted to be if he applied himself.

As they approached the tall Johnson grass, Billy Ray knew a shortcut to Mary Jo's house. He found out about it one day, when he just kept going through the tall grass and found himself in front of her house. This grass was so high that you could not see the top of their heads. It was like a jungle, very dense with very little sunlight coming through.

After walking up to the grass B. J. wanted to know what Billy Ray saw. Using his imagination, Billy Ray began to tell about his adventure in the tall Johnson grass. "The tall grass is a wild jungle where tigers, lions, elephants live; a place where monkeys swing through the tall grass," Billy Ray said smiling.

"Really cry baby!" B. J. said. They both laughed and went into the tall grass.

CHAPTER XXVI
AFRICAN JUNGLE HUNT

The boys pretended that they were looking for tigers and elephants in Africa. They were on an adventure and knew that they were downwind from any animals. This meant that the tigers or other animals could not smell them either.

B.J. and Billy Ray crouched down waiting for a tiger to leap out of the tree. Billy Ray told B.J. that he was really smart. "Huh!" B. J. did not want to make any noise, so he shook his head in agreeing to Billy Ray's statement.

Billy Ray saw two sticks on the ground and picked them up. "Huh!" Billy Ray softly said, "These will make fine hunting rifles." He noticed the pretend tiger getting ready to leap out of the tree.

"Bang, Bang," B. J. said, as Billy Ray pretended to be the tiger. Immediately, B. J. ran over and put his foot on his prize. He was proud of his kill, as he picked up his head right between the eyes. "Un! He will make a nice trophy huh, friend."

Billy Ray could not help but laugh at B. J. acting as if he had really made a big kill. Billy Ray reached up and grabbed B. J. by the leg. He tripped and fell down beside him to the ground. They stayed in the jungle talking and laughing about how Billy Ray would be daydreaming out the school window. He would be lost when the teacher asked him a question.

Still forgetting about the time, B. J. and Billy Ray spent another hour in the tall grass. B.J. said they needed to get going. "Oops," Billy Ray said, "I know it is time for us to meet up with Mary Jo."

B.J. moaning "Ooh!" The boys knew they were in for it now. Knowing how Mary Jo's behavior is, the boys knew they were in big trouble. The boys went through that tall grass, as if a bear was on their tail. You could see the tall grass swaying as they ran through each section. B. J. and Billy Ray reached the opening and saw Mary Jo pacing up and down the road in front of her house.

"Well! Look what the cat drug in," Mary Jo said. "Where have you two been? You know we have to go by the twins' house." Billy Ray and B.J. looked as if they were her two boys that got caught acting bad.

Neither of the boys chose to say anything. They continued to listen to Mary Jo rant and rave about them not coming earlier. Billy Ray and B. J. smiled at Mary Jo because they wanted to go to the movies. These boys were willing to do anything Mary Jo wanted them to do. They were not going to say anything that would make her madder.

In other words, the boys were afraid to answer Mary Jo. Once she got started, she did not know when to stop talking. "Huh!" B. J. silently said, "that girl should run for president, they need a talker like her."

In the meantime, B.J. was still trying to convince Mary Jo why they were late. B.J. took a chance and said, "Mary Jo, it was very hot walking over here, so we took a break to cool down. Billy Ray and I sat under a tree for a while. And, and you know people get one of those things from the sun (sun stroke) huh, Billy Ray."

Billy Ray did not know what to do so he shook his head instead of saying anything. "See, see, I told you Mary Jo," B.J. said, trying to defend his case.

Billy Ray looked confused as he looked up in the sky. "What thing from the sun?" B. J. nudged Billy Ray and tried to wink his eye that he was just playing. Flyboy continued to look up in the sky and B. J. got very agitated with him. Nevertheless, all B. J. wanted to do was just go.

Anyway, why was Mary Jo acting as if she was Charley Chan from the movies, asking fifty questions? Putting her hands on those two bony hips she looked strangely at B. J and Billy Ra. She was ready to go. While walking towards the twin's house, Billy Ray's conscience began to bother him. He suddenly stopped and told Mary Jo "The reason we were late was because we went swimming."

B. J. was dumbfounded, as he could not believe Billy Ray came up with such a fantastic story. B. J. did not dare tell a lie, even if he said it in his mind. That definitely was a no, no. He quickly backed Billy Ray up saying "Yeah, that's why we were late Mary Jo."

Mary Jo gave B. J. and Billy Ray, one of those evil eyed looks and said, "lest get the twins."

In addition to being who she is, Mary Jo said, "B. J. and Billy Ray how come y'all clothes are not wet huh?"

B. J. put his hand over his mouth and tried to think of something to say fast. "You know, Mary Jo it is about a hundred degrees out here and if we stay out here too long, we are going to dry up too." B. J. thought, *boy you are a genius for coming up with such a great answer.*

Nevertheless, B. J. must have forgotten Mary Jo was also just as smart as he was. She quickly said, "B. J. Perkins Jr., you need to be ashamed of yourself. You do not dry up from walking in the sun. And this is not," as she put her hands on those hips of hers, "Sahara Desert."

"Do you see any sand dunes around here huh, B. J. Perkins?" Oh, B. J. was smart this time as he walked down the road not saying another word to that girl. He thought, *where does she get all that stuff she knows? Huh! She is just too brainy for me.*

Billy Ray was still bothered about not telling Mary Jo the truth. He realized that he just told a big fib, even if he did not say anything, he agreed with B. J. All he wanted to know was whether or not Mary Jo was still taking them to the movies. He had to get back in good graces with her.

Undaunted, Billy Ray walked up beside Mary Jo and said, "Uh, ah, Mary Jo where are we going when we get the twins?"

Mary Jo was perturbed as she popped her lips and said, "We are going to the movies, Billy Ray," as she stood looking at him eye to eye.

One would have thought that a horse was bucking Billy Ray, as he yelled out "Wow! Yippee!"

"Didn't you tell him we all are going to the movies?" Mary Jo asked. He was acting like a kid with a tootsie-roll- pop.

"UN! Yea-ah Mary Jo, I did" B. J. said.

Billy Ray was into himself, as he stood back on his legs, stuck out his chest, put his hands on his hips, and tried to say in a deep voice, "The new action movie is Stagecoach War, with Hop-Along Cassidy and his horse Thunder." Billy Ray shouted, "playing today, folks."

Mary Jo was not impressed with Billy Ray's act but did say, "Hum, that's nice, Billy Ray."

"UH, Huh, Uh Huh, Mary Jo, thanks," Billy Ray breathlessly said.

Mary Jo thought, *I do not remember Hop-Along Cassidy's horse being named Thunder. It's Topper.* She shook her head and thought this kid had been to too many movies.

Billy Ray really blew it when he told Mary Jo (the movie queen) "It was nice of you to take us to the movies."

B.J. was not very impressed with what Billy Ray was talking about, after that mean thing Mary Jo said and did to him at the fish fry. Most men and boys seem to hold on to things that are done to them. On the other hand, they want the girls and women to act as if it never happened.

B.J. quickly tore that speech of Mary Jo's down and took that tiara right off of the queen's head when he said, "Well it is our money too, Billy Ray. Mary Jo's mama had a big fish fry for us, and Mrs. Hattie gave us part of the money."

"Oh Yeah! B. J." Mary Jo looked surprised, as she tried to whisper so Billy Ray could not hear what she was saying. "You have a big mouth, B. J. I wanted it to be a big surprise for Billy Ray."

Wanting to convince Mary Jo that Billy Ray is still happy. B. J. said, "Look! Look!" as he pointed to Billy Ray, "see he's happy. He is over there in the hot sun acting as if he is a cowboy. Mary Jo he is surprised."

"Well!" Mary Jo dryly said, "I guess Billy Ray was surprised."

It was time to go as Mary Jo told them, "Come on. I wasted enough time on you boys." Following Mary Jo, B.J. was mocking her with the different gestures she made. Billy Ray could not help but laugh at B. J. as Mary Jo turned around and almost caught him. B.J. quickly looked up at the sky and pretended he was so hot. She said, "Um, I do not know why I put up with you boys."

B. J., grinning, said "Hey, Mary Jo, when did the twins get back?"

Mary Jo, being at her best, said, "Am I to know everything B. J., because I'm smart huh?"

"Uh, aha, that is why I asked you, Mary Jo because you are smarty….Oops! I meant smart" Mary Jo was frustrated with these boys. After all, God did not give them the nice things like he did the girls. Mary Jo grimaced and said, "the twins came back Tuesday night."

B. J. sternly said, "And, and, how come you did not say anything the other day? Huh, Mary Jo?"

Mary Jo, looking pious said, "Cause B.J. you did not ask me, and I did not think that it was that important to you boys," as she stood with her hand on her bony hip moving from side to side.

B. J. quickly let Miss Important know that they missed the twins too "Huh! Billy Ray?" During this time, Billy Ray did not want to set this girl off, so he just shook his head and did not respond. All he wanted to do was go to the movies.

CHAPTER XXVII
WHERE ARE THE BOYS?

As expected, Mary Jo wanted answers as to why the boys were late. She noticed that the cockle berries in their hair and on the back of their tee shirts. B. J. thought, *we have let this girl trick us again by changing the subject.* Billy Ray looked to B.J. to tell Mary Jo where the cockle berries came from.

B.J. politely walked ahead of Billy Ray and Mary Jo. He refused to say anything else to this girl. He figured he'd let Billy Ray tell her the reason why they were late. Billy Ray had enough, as he was always the one talking for B.J.

Billy Ray could not take Mary Jo's badgering anymore. He told Mary Jo they did not go swimming, like he said. He included the part where they were crying as if they were two babies needing a bottle.

Nevertheless, fate has a way of softening anyone's heart and Mary Jo was no exception. After hearing the boys' story, Mary Jo gingerly kissed Billy Ray and B. J. on their foreheads. The motherly part played an important part in her as she always acted as if she was their second mama. She let the boys know how proud she was of both of them.

Billy Ray let Mary Jo know she could have laughed, because that is what they did afterwards. "In other words, Mary Jo," Billy Ray said, "we laugh at each other, huh, B. J." This was the boy's moment of relief, and it was alright to cry. The boys will always share this special moment. Mary Jo did not want to laugh as she walked ahead of the boys, leaving them alone for a while.

Looking as if he missed the point, Billy Ray said, "Why do girls think that boys do not cry huh, B. J.?"

"Probably because Mary Jo got that from her mama, Billy Ray," B. J. said. "Our nicknames are going to be crybabies."

"Ah shucks, B.J." Billy Ray said. "Who cares if she calls us crybabies. It ain't true huh?"

"Well Billy Ray, it is good to cry because it's a good way to wash out your eyeballs."

"Wow! B. J. How did you learn that?"

B.J. said, "Because I enjoy reading books."

Bill Ray was astonished as he said, "Oh!" B.J., you are really a bookworm huh?" Billy Ray was so amazed to learn that crying washes your eyeballs out.

Mary Jo looked back and noticed the boys still talking. She thought, *I feel silly for forcing the boys to tell me why they were late.* The boys' feelings and the love they shared with each other touched Mary Jo's heart. She felt that Billy Ray needed a friend such as B. J. She knew he'd bring out the good qualities that are inside ready to be discovered.

She yelled for the boys to come along, if they wanted to go to the movies. Mary Jo decided to take the weight off of her feet and sit by the roadside. The boys were sure to be coming down the road soon. She leaned back on the grass and mulled over what to do about getting Billy Ray a gift.

Finally, the boys walked up to where Mary Jo was getting up and dusting her pants off. At that moment, Billy Ray noticed something on her shirt. Billy Ray called out, "Hey! Mary Jo, what, what, is that crawling up your back!? Huh!"

Knowing how the boys enjoy playing little tricks on her, Mary Jo did not pay much attention to what Billy Ray was talking about. She posed as she asked, "How do I know Billy Ray? Do I have eyes in the back of my head? I think not. It would help if you did, because you could tell me what it is."

"Oh, turn around, Mary Jo. I'll take it off." He carefully took the snail off and held it in his hand to show Mary Jo. "See," B. J. said, "It is just a harmless snail." Mary Jo started jumping up and down as if she was in church, feeling the spirit.

She was yelling so loud that people could hear her on the next road. "Get that nasty thing away from me right now, B.J. Just kill it." If it was left up to this girl, there would not be any animals, or insects left.

B J. gently laid the snail back in the grass and quieted Mary Jo down. The lab scientist said, "It is all right now, Mary Jo." She sprouted about the little harmless snail. B.J. pointed his finger at her saying, "That snail did not like it, Mary Jo." This seemed to get her attention as she said, "Yeah, you are so right B.J."

"Oo-oo-oh," Mary Jo said, as she walked past where B. J. had just put the snail down. Billy Ray did not seem to care one way or another. All he wanted was to get to the picture show.

After gaining her composure again, Mary Jo nonchalantly said, "Oh boys, after the movie I will take the twins home."

B. J. feeling proud of himself, said, "Oh no! Mary Jo, we cannot let you do that huh, Billy Ray? Shucks no! Mary Jo."

Billy Ray said, "All the stuff you are doing for us today, Mary Jo; taking us to the movie."

Quickly, Mary Jo said "Excuse us, Billy Ray. I need to talk with B.J. for a moment."

They walked to the other side of the road leaving B. J. standing there, wondering what was going on. Look, B. J.," Mary Jo said sharply. "I need you to be with Billy Ray."

"What for Mary Jo?" B.J. loudly asked. "We can walk you and the girls home."

In the meantime, Billy Ray was across the road looking at Mary Jo with a confused look on his face. She and B. J. were yelling at each other. *Huh*, Billy Ray thought, "*there they go at it again fusing at each other. What are they talking about now?* Billy Ray began to wonder, as he shifted from one foot to the other.

Mary Jo was at her wits end. She finally whispered that the girls were going to get Billy Ray a gift after the movies. She needed B. J. to go home with Billy Ray, so the girls could go shopping. Mary Jo wanted to pick out something nice that Billy Ray would enjoy.

"Oh!" as B.J. hit his forehead, as if someone turned on his light. He finally understood what Mary Jo wanted to do. "That is why you want Billy Ray and me to go home. That is a good idea, Mary Jo."

Mary Jo, feeling herself as a good leader, proudly put her hands on those two bony hips swaying from side to side. B. J. refused to say another word to this girl. He knows how she will go on and on. It was not enough time for her to be a star right now. They need to hurry up and get the twins.

B. J. asked Mary Jo, "Where'd you get all the stuff, you know huh?" B. J. did not realize that he opened another can of worms. She was still standing with her hands on her hips, swaying.

Mary Jo replied, "God made us girls smart so that we can help you boys." As she walked away with a stern look on her face, she said, "Let's go!" in a demanding tone. B. J. heard what she just said, however, he did not know how much of it was true.

In the meantime, Billy Ray was wondering whether Mary Jo had changed her mind about the movies. He noticed how she took off walking down the road without B. J. Billy Ray was getting anxious about what happened between B. J. and Mary Jo.

As Mary Jo walked past Billy Ray, he politely asked her if he did something wrong. "Oh no Billy Ray," Mary Jo bluntly responded. She told Billy Ray she had to tell B. J. about something he did yesterday.

Billy Ray had a big smile on his face, as B. J. put his arm on Billy Ray's shoulder. "Everything is alright now, partner."

CHAPTER XXVIII
GOING TO GET THE TWINS

Hurrying down the road, the gang could see the twin's house from the corner. B.J. and Billy Ray said, "Pooh! It's hot."

Mary Jo said, "Yeah and my feet are hot." She promptly sat down and took off her sandals. It was overcast that day, so the sun was behind the clouds, but this made the sun even hotter. The queen decided she needed to rest for a minute.

B.J. wiped the sweat from his face and looked at Mary Jo, wondering why she was sitting down? *We still have to go and get the twins,* B. J. thought and there was Mary Jo, sitting as if she was the Queen."

Mary Jo was no dummy. She sensed what the boys were thinking and waved her hand for them to go. She continued to rub her feet and slowly got up from the curb. The hot sun made her wish for a cold glass of water. She quickly put her sandals on.

She had a thought, as she sat back down. *Why should I have to go and get the twins?* She said, "B. J. and Billy Ray, y'all can go get the twins. I will just wait here," as she found some shade under a tree.

"Aha!" Mary Jo said as a cool breeze crossed her face. She thought, *I need this time to figure out how much money to give the gang.*

Not really paying attention to the boys, Mary Jo leaned back and enjoyed that moment to think. Looking up from where she was sitting Mary Jo said loudly, "Just because you made me stand out in the hot sun waiting for you, y'all go and get the twins." Mary Jo laid back under the tree to rest until the boys came back.

The boys stood there looking like two little lost sheep that could not find their mama. They could not believe she just said that. Mary Jo knew that would stir up the boys and without a doubt they would not refuse.

During this time, Billy Ray was praying that B. J. did not say anything that would upset this girl. Billy Ray really wanted to go to the movies to see one of his favorite cowboy characters and B.J. saw the look on his face. He decided not to say anything.

Mary Jo is really making us almost beg her to take us to the movies. Huh! B. J. thought. *After all, I had to take her tongue-lashing, hot-air breath and finger-pointing self. She just carried her leadership a little too far today, so she can stand on her soapbox.*

Billy Ray was standing as if he was a cowboy again trying to hold his mouth as if he was his favorite cowboy. "What a man has to go through just to be a man, huh, Billy Ray thought?" Nothing was going to change so they decided to go and get the twins.

"Ah! Come on Billy Ray. Let's go and get the twins," B. J. said, as they walked down the block. Looking down the street, they could see the little figures on the porch. It was the twins anxiously waiting for the gang to come and get them. Billy Ray and B. J. hurried toward the house, waving their hands.

This gave Mary Jo a chance to think about what to get Billy Ray. Her mama gave her enough of the money they made to buy a nice gift. She could see Billy Ray's face as she made her big speech in front of the gang. They would all look up to her for the great adventures she planned for them this summer. After all, she is the smartest in the gang, besides B.J. On the other hand, Billy Ray, bless his heart, has his head too much in the clouds. "Now, how could he think or come up with a good idea? Oh! Yes, yes, the twins. What do they have to offer?" Mary Jo laughed. The twins enjoy asking twenty questions.

B. J. is too smart for his own good. He is a walking book that knows a little about everything. For the most part, he knows about different types of insects, birds, lizards, bugs, and whatever he can learn from reading books. Mary Jo gave the history behind each of her little people. What a group of kids to lead.

Nevertheless, Mary Jo enjoyed every moment they were together. B. J. and Mary Jo are only children. These kids make up for her and B. J. not knowing the joys and, sometimes problems, of having siblings. This day was going to be filled with fun and things for the little group to do. Giving the gang part of the money from the fish fry was going to be a big treat. They can pay their way into the movies and still have ninety cents left.

Now, Billy Ray won't have to stop at the candy counter, wishing he could buy a candy bar. Mary Jo is giving each one of them some money to spend. She was so proud of herself knowing they chose the right person to be their leader and planner.

In the meantime, Billy Ray and B. J. were in a hurry to get to the twins house. The twins were anxiously pacing back and forth in the hallway and on the porch, peeping out the screen door and walking up and down the steps. Looking and feeling disgusted, the twins could have worn a hole in their porch as much walking as they did.

Because of the low hanging limbs on the trees, the twins could not see up to the corner. They needed to walk out to the end of the sidewalk to see. Their neighbor had a big Oak tree in their yard too. In the summertime, the tree played an important part in providing shade and a cool breeze. Most people did not have those big swamp fans, but the twins had one in their house.

Half-heartedly, Shirley said, "What's taking them so long, huh Sandy?"

This made Sandy really mad, "I do not know Shirley and stop pestering me," Sandy harshly said.

It is hot and the twins had a right to be at each other's throats. There are some kids on the street but most of them are teenagers, which means they do not have time for two talkative twins. For the most part, Mary Jo, Billy Ray, and B. J. are the only little people to play with around their neighborhood, even though they live a little far from B. J., Billy Ray and Mary Jo. Most likely, that is the reason their mother let the twins go places with the little gang.

Suddenly, the twins heard someone calling their names. The joy came back into their little faces, as the boys came to get them. Shirley jumped up and down on the porch while Sandy was getting up from the steps saying "Yeah! The boys are here." The twins did not have to tell Mabel that they were going; she was happy for them.

B.J. and Billy Ray ran through the gate and up to the porch steps. "Hi twins, it has been a long time since we have been together, huh? How was your vacation?" B. J. asked.

Shirley and Sandy, overly excited, said, "we had fun, fun, fun and more fun. We did not forget the gang. We brought each of you a present."

Billy Ray and B.J. all keyed up and forgetting that they were thirsty said, "Oh yeah! Really twins? What did you bring us?" Shirley told them to wait, and she would be right back. She went through the screen door so fast, as if something was after her.

The boys were so excited, they were nodding their heads like mockingbirds. While she was in the house, Billy Ray kept his eyes glued to the front door. *No one ever brought me a gift*, he thought.

You could hear Shirley running down the hallway and out the door. She had a shopping bag. She reached into the bag and carefully gave Billy Ray his gift and said, "I hope you like it."

Just like a kid on Christmas, he quickly tore the paper off the package. He had an amazed look in his eyes. His face was aglow, and you could hear the excitement in his voice. "Gee whiz!" Billy Ray said. "This is the best gift that I ever got. How did y'all know this is what I always wanted?"

It was a model airplane. The twins looked at each other and whispered, "Hum, most of his conversations are about airplanes."

Laughing, the twins said, "We are glad you like it, Billy Ray."

Noticing his friend's expression and his eyes getting watery, B. J. told Billy Ray, "We did enough of that this morning huh?"

Billy Ray quickly wiped his eyes, not wanting the twins to start crying too. Shirley walked over and put her arms around Billy Ray to comfort him. She could see and feel how much Billy Ray liked his gift. Once again, Billy Ray wiped his eyes. He just held on to his airplane, as if it may fly away.

B. J. was getting excited as the twins gave him his gift. He could not believe his eyes as he tore open the paper. "Wow!" B. J. shouted, "look at this, Billy Ray." He held his gift up so Billy Ray could see it better. Billy Ray was so elated by what his eyes were seeing. In the package was a beautiful butterfly encased in a wooden frame.

Shirley smiled and said, "B. J., you can add this to your other collections that you have in your lab."

He stood there in awe, as he gazed at the lovely gift the twins brought him. This butterfly was hard to come by. Billy Ray was so happy for his friend. "The twins picked each of us a precious gift that will last," Billy Ray said. "Twins, we cannot thank you enough."

CHAPTER XXIX
THE TWIN'S GIFT TO THEIR FRIENDS

Now that the twins had given the boys their gift it was time to go. They loudly cleared their throats to break up the over-thrilled boys. They simultaneously said, "B. J. and Billy Ray, we need to go before Mary Jo comes looking for us."

The boys eagerly said, "Ok, twins!" The twins let the boys know they would give Mary Jo her gift.

They all walked back up the street to get Mary Jo and continue on to the movies. The little gang found Mary Jo sitting on the curb in deep thought. She raised her head and noticed the twins through the heart waves. She waved from afar. The twins were grinning from ear to ear as they approached Mary Jo.

"Hi, Mary Jo!" The twins shouted when they saw her. Sandy and Shirley gave her a big hug to let her know how much they missed her.

"Look, look, Mary Jo," Billy Ray said, as he showed her the new airplane the twins gave him. "This is what the twins gave me," he said, as he held out his new airplane.

"What did they give you B. J.?" Mary Jo asked. She decided to look at the boys' gift first before opening her own.

Taking her time, she looked at Billy Ray's airplane and B. J.'s beautiful butterfly. She could see how much Billy Ray was enjoying that nice airplane. Billy Ray was acting like a kid with his teddy bear at bedtime. Mary Jo, playing the mother role again, told Billy Ray not to break it, but that was far from Billy Ray's mind. He could name every part of that plane while taking it apart and putting it back together again.

The twins were waiting patiently for Mary Jo to open the bag with her gift inside. She had the opportunity to look at the boys' gifts. Why was she taking so long? The boys had all kinds of negative thoughts running through their brains. Nevertheless, it seemed as if she did not want what the twins bought her. Sometimes it is just hard to know how that brain of hers is working.

The boys' gifts seemed to be more important to her than her own gift. The twins also noticed her actions. After pacifying the boy's ego as if they needed it, Mary Jo decided it was time for her to see. She knew the twins wanted her to open the bag, so she peeped inside slowly, as if she was pulling out a snake that was ready to strike.

As she reached down, she picked up a beautiful ebony doll. This doll had big curly locks of black hair. She had a pink bow on the top of her head tied onto a curly lock. She had big, glass brown eyes with long, black curled up eyelashes, a pug nose and rosy cheeks. She also had a little red on her lips. The color of the dress was pink. There was a white pinafore over the dress that was tied in the back. She had on white shoes and pink ruffle socks with white lace around the top. Mary Jo was just like the boys about her gift, thrilled that the twins would buy her such a lovely gift.

"Oh! Thank you twins! She is so pretty. Look at the beautiful dress she has on. Thank you again, twins. This is so nice of y'all."

The twins were all smiles and delighted that the gang loved their gifts. The twins told the gang that they have a doll like Mary Jo's too. Shirley's doll has a yellow dress and Sandy's, a blue dress. The twins said, "Mary Jo, maybe we can playhouse when you come and bring your doll." Mary Jo thought that was a good idea.

Now that everyone had received their gifts from the twins, it was time to go. Mary Jo and the twins need to put that dumb doll back in the bag because the picture show is not going to wait. Besides, the sun had a tendency to get hotter in the afternoons, and this day was no exception. B. J. was hot, as he shuffled from one foot to the other. He was trying to get the twins' attention but to no avail. He was ready to go.

He stared at the girls as they had girl talk. B. J. knew boys do not like dolls so "Why are we boys standing here getting hotter?" You could not convince Billy Ray of that fact. This boy was right in the conversation with the girls talking about those dolls. B. J. had had enough, and his patience had grown thin as he yelled, "Hey! Aren't you ready to go to the movies?"

Nevertheless, Billy Ray waved his hand and showed very little concern about the movies. The girls seemed mesmerized by these silly dolls. B. J. walked over, took the doll and Billy Ray's plane and put them back in the bag. They quickly got the message and continued down the road.

Mary Jo intentionally stalled for time with the girls. She needed to talk with the girls about the fish fry, but felt it was more important to talk about the cowboy outfit. The twins looked confused and dumbfounded and did not know about any cowboy outfit. They were somewhat afraid to ask any questions. They looked at Mary Jo wondering what she was talking about. She popped her lips and batted her eyes, as she revealed her plan to the twins. You can bet the twins had a lot of questions for Mary Jo. Just as quick as Mary Jo told them her plan, they came up with a different question. Sandy asked, "Why are we not on our way to the movies huh Mary Jo?" Mary Jo was not surprised at her question, and she seemed to need an answer. She just took the twins' hands and hurried down the road.

After walking so fast, she stopped, paused, and took a deep breath. She was acting as if she just ran a track meet. This was her golden moment as she stood there on her soapbox. It has been a while since she has had an opportunity to speak to the twins or the boys.

Mary Jo was now ready for her big speech, and she definitely had the twins' attention. She had to point out four things the twins needed to know. "First, of all twins," Mary Jo said, "we had a fish fry that my mama suggested for B. J. and me to do." Then she went through all of the things that the two of them did to make money for Billy Ray.

During this time, Mary Jo did not stop long enough for the twins to ask any questions. Finally, Mary Jo got to the last thing on her list, Billy Ray's gift and what to buy him. Mary Jo told them her mama suggested that the gang buy Billy Ray a cowboy outfit. The twins said, suspiciously, "Huh! That's nice, but what do you think, Mary Jo?"

Scolding the twins, she said, "I thought my mama's idea was great."

"Oh! Is that so, Mary Jo?" the twins nonchalantly said. "I thought my mama's idea was great." She continued, to talk about her mama cooking all the fish. The sandwiches sold for thirty-five cents each. Using her fingers, Mary Jo showed the twins that they had made enough money. One, they could go to the movies; Two, they each could get a treat; Three they could buy Billy Ray a nice gift.

The twins' suspicion quickly changed their demeanor when they found out that Mary Jo was giving each one of them a whole dollar. This is the reason Mary Jo told the twins they needed the boys to go home. The girls had to go shopping at the five and dime store. Smiling, the twins agreed with Mary Jo as they continued down the road to the movie show.

In the meantime, Sandy was not at all satisfied with the money because Mary Jo still did not tell them how much they had made. Sandy had mulled it over in her mind and wondered why it was such a big secret. "How much did Mary Jo make?" she wondered.

Having a sixth sense, Shirley shared the same thought as her twin Sandy. She came right out and wanted to know how much they had made. This floored Mary Jo, as she looked at the twins in disbelief that they would ask such a question. They were not even here, and she is sharing it with the little brats.

"Well! I never," Mary Jo said, as she wiped the sweat from her forehead. "These two little brats have the nerve to ask me a question again. Where were they at when B. J. and I had to go find junk to sell for the fish fry? They were off somewhere enjoying their vacation with their parents," Mary Jo said to herself.

She thought, *this takes the cake that the baker dropped. Huh*, as she stood with her hands on her hips, rocking back and forth. We all know where Mary Jo got that. She decided to let the twins know how much each of them would get. Everybody, including the twins, would get a dollar for the movies and the rest would go towards buying Billy Ray a cowboy outfit.

Nonetheless, the twins were a menace. They interrupted Mary Jo again saying, "A whole dollar?"

"Yeah!" Mary Jo replied. With all of those words said, Mary Jo still did not reveal to the twins how much money they made. The twins gave a look but decided not to ask about anything else since they each would receive a whole dollar for the movies. It did not matter too much anyway at this point. They were all in a happy place.

You don't want to miss what my friends and I did in my next adventure book, The Happy Place.